Before and After Freedom

Before and After Freedom

Freedom

Lowcountry Folklore and Narratives

NANCY RHYNE

Charleston   London

History
PRESS

Published by The History Press
18 Percy Street
Charleston, SC 29403
866.223.5778
www.historypress.net

Cover photograph courtesy of the Historic American Building Survey, 1937.

First published 2005

Manufactured in the United Kingdom

ISBN 1.59629.086.2

Library of Congress Cataloging-in-Publication Data

Before and after freedom : WPA narratives of Lowcountry folklore / [compiled
by] Nancy Rhyne.
    p. cm.
  Includes index.
  ISBN 1-59629-086-2 (alk. paper)
  1. African Americans--South Carolina--Folklore. 2. Freedmen--South
Carolina--Folklore. 3. Tales--South Carolina. 4. Legends--South Carolina.
5. United States. Works Progress Administration. South Carolina. I. Rhyne,
Nancy, 1926-
  GR111.A47B44 2005
  398.2'089'960730757--dc22
                         2005022179

Notice: The information in this book is true and complete to the best of our knowledge.
It is offered without guarantee on the part of the author or The History Press. The
author and The History Press disclaim all liability in connection with the use of this
book.

This book is dedicated to Garry and Shirlene Rhyne. They know why.

Contents

Preface

In the late 1930s the Writer's Project of the U.S. Works Progress Administration (WPA) collected South Carolina history and legends on a comprehensive scale. As a result of the five and a half years of work, which covered practically every county in the state, a gratifyingly large and interesting body of folklore has been accumulated. Each former slave had a story that needed to be told and when approached by the WPA field workers, the tales came pouring out. In all, the collection runs to thousands of written pages. In addition to the originals, filed in the Library of Congress, a copy of the material, which so intimately concerns the past traditions and the unwritten folk culture of South Carolina, is stored in the South Caroliniana branch of the University Library and can be readily and freely consulted by all interested persons.

Before and After Freedom is an assembly of this Lowcountry folklore and much more. As well as consulting the WPA narratives for days and weeks upon end, my husband Sid and I spent many glorious hours in slave cabins, African Methodist Episcopal churches and some historic mansions, interviewing the children and "grands" of former slaves because not every person who had a story to tell was contacted by a field worker of the WPA. For me, the path of selecting the stories was much the same as when I add my personal touch to a revered recipe. I usually throw in one or two of my favorite ingredients to add my mark to the concoction. So to the selected stories from the WPA files, I have also included personal interviews and other historical narratives of this region. While every story in this book does not include the subject of slavery, they all include the subject of the Lowcounty. All of the WPA field workers' text is in its original form, and if available the WPA field worker's name, interview locations and date are also included.

Before and After Freedom

In an earlier century when these storytellers lived in cabins in the slavequarters, they told tales to their children and to their children's children, and eventually the stories almost told themselves. The characters were quite different in the children's stories. Genevieve Willcox Chandler of Murrells Inlet, South Carolina, was one of the greatest field workers the WPA ever had. She said that long before Joel Chandler Harris wrote his Uncle Remus stories, the slaves on the coast of South Carolina made up their own animal scenarios. The hero of the tale was a creature of some intelligence and complexity and the tale taught a lesson not to be forgotten. The animal stories became known as "trickster tales," and I have included some of them in this book.

Likewise, I have added to this book several tales that were personally told to me by people who lived in remote areas and never gave an interview until I came along. Sue Alston, a daughter of slaves, who became the housekeeper at Archibald Rutledge's home of Hampton Plantation, lived to the age of 110 and was lucid until the time of her death. She always had a story for us. Miss Corrie Dusenbury, an elegant lady who lived until her death in a waterfront home in Murrells Inlet, uttered graphic tales of hurricanes and her life on this coast during another century. Though their tales were not found among the WPA manuscripts, they are certainly not less important. We visited aristocrats, historians and Lowcountry residents who had their own versions of this period of our history and contributed their narratives of events and places. In their recollections, everything is a subject. A subject can involve your emotions, your impressions and your presence of nature.

By the standards of society today, these narrators are small-time, and wouldn't even be represented by a notch on a tree. We tend to forget how the shriveled and meager ones achieved their goals and became a rather large bump on a log. They had in themselves that which is truly honorable, but rarely did they think about it. The people mentioned in this book were coastal dwellers and a large portion of this collection has been written in the Gullah dialect, a strange and unique language. It is difficult for an outsider to understand much of the language due to odd emphasis, pronunciation and numerous idioms. An attempt has been made to render the conversation as clearly as possible for the average reader as well as retain the true meaning of the story.

May my faithful readers enjoy the tales of the South Carolina saints who march through this collection.

Nancy Rhyne
Columbia, South Carolina

Living in Heaven

I belonged to Maussa Seabrook. He lived at White Point, about ten miles from Adams Run.

I be Baptist. I be baptized in the Edisto River. I be a-tryin' to get to Heaven. Heaven be glory. You got to love all God's chillun to get there. God send white folks and colored folks and they must help each other and work together. They've got to live in union. That's what the folks, white and colored, are doing in Heaven. Living in union.

John Hamilton
As told to Gyland H. Hamlin, WPA field worker.
Charleston, South Carolina 1937.

An Accident of God

I'm Ben Horry. I been borned at Brookgreen Plantation, in Murrells Inlet.

One day I had a boat full of people. Miss Mary, her auntie, and more. I rowed them halfway to Drunken Jack Island. [Drunken Jack Island washed away during the storm that crashed on South Carolina's shore Friday, the 13th of October 1893. Drunken Jack once was an island of wealth and glory. It once was the site of the Hot and Hot Fish Club, and a place rice planters visited for what they called "convivial and social intercourse." It was named for a pirate named Jacque, a drunkard who died there and was buried behind a sand dune.]

Water splash in. Breakers start to lick the people. I start to bail the boat. It been dangerous 'cause all were women in there. Boat turn over. All dumped into the water. I couldn't help them. Decided to swim and save myself. And then it happened by accident. Our feet touched the bottom. Everybody walked to shore. Only an accident from God.

Ben Horry
As told to Genevieve W. Chandler, WPA field worker.
Murrells Inlet, South Carolina 1937.

The Mere-Maid (Mermaid)

I, Ben Horry, be the oldest liver on the Waccamaw Neck. Live on Joshua John Ward's plantation, Brookgreen. 'Fore freedom? Well, 'fore freedom we were treated good. Maussa Josh's daughter marry Dr. Arthur Flagg, and they have son, Dr. J. Ward Flagg. In that day and time the Wards have house on Magnolia Beach.

Dr. J. Ward Flagg caught a mere-maid in a fishing net. He shut up mere-maid in a shack behind his house on Magnolia Beach. Everyone knows that when a mere-maid is shut up, rain will come and the water level will rise and wash the mere-maid back to her home in the sea.

We say, "Dr. Flagg. Let that mere-maid loose." He say, "I don't have a mere-maid."

We looked through a hole in the wall and watched mere-maid slide across the floor. She was pretty people. As pretty people as you ever see. All scales from waist down. Slide along on a fish tail.

I go there now and talk to Dr. Flagg 'bout that storm what come when he keep the mere-maid shut up. Dr. Flagg's eyes get full of water. He lost thirteen head of his family in the storm what come to free mere-maid. He wouldn't listen. Wouldn't free mere-maid. Tide came and got her and took her back to sea.

Ben Horry
As told to Genevieve W. Chandler, WPA field worker.
Murrells Inlet, South Carolina 1937.

A Hiding Place

I was born in Rebel Time on a plantation down by Beaufort. It was a scary time but I found me a hiding place. I was a little gal when they shoot the big guns on Fort Sumter. With the troubulation and bombation I had to stand up to, you cannot blame me for forgetting the name of the plantation where I was born. It was near Beaufort.

I want to go to heaven now, and when the roll is called, the Lord will find a hiding place for me in heaven.

Emma Fraser
As told to C.R. Tiedeman, WPA field worker.
Charleston, South Carolina 1937.

Buh Patridge and Buh Rabbit

Buh Patridge met Buh Rabbit in the woods. It was raining. Buh Patridge have he head under he wing. He gone right on walking and had head under he arm.

Buh Rabbit say, "Buh Patridge, what you doing out here in the rain with your head off?"

Buh Patridge say, "Buh Rabbit, when it raining, I allus cuts my head off and leaves it at home. Then my head don't never get wet."

Buh Rabbit stand and drop he mouth open and look at Buh Patridge and then gone running on home in the rain. When he get home, he say, "Old lady, I want you to cut off my head."

Mrs. Rabbit say, "Cut off your head! You'll be dead." "No. I met Buh Patridge in the rain today with his head cut off and he didn't dead." And Buh Rabbit kept on pestering Mrs. Rabbit till she take the axe and Buh Rabbit put he head down on the block and she come ker whack.

Here Buh Rabbit head cut clean off from the body. Kick a little. Flutter about. He dead.

Wife went to crying.

Buh Patridge off in the bushes. He know what happened and came a-singing, "Hey, old lady, where Buh Rabbit?"

Old Mrs. Rabbit show 'em.

Buh Patridge laugh and say, "Great God. That old fool ain't know I had my head under my wing.

Mrs. Rabbit didn't think that was very funny.

Zackie Knox
As told to Genevieve W. Chandler, WPA field worker.
Murrells Inlet, South Carolina 1937.

Sheep Heads and Dumpling

One time a man killed some sheep. An old woman and her son, who lived nearby, helped him. The man who owned the sheep gave the woman a piece of meat in gratitude for her help, but she did not want the meat. She wanted all the sheep heads. The man gave her all of them, and it was almost more than she and her son could carry home.

The woman cleaned the sheep heads and skinned them. The next morning, just before she got ready to go to church, she put the sheep heads in a large pot. She covered the heads in water, brought the water to a boil, and added some dumplings. She got dressed, and as she went out the door, she cautioned her son not to let the pot boil over.

The boy kept watch over the pot. After the sheep heads started to boil, he saw them turning over and over in the pot. He believed the sheep were trying to bump the dumplings out of the pot. The boy thought he had better run to the church and tell his mama that the sheep were butting the dumplings out of the pot.

He spotted his mama sitting at the end of a pew near the door. The boy called his mama's name. She turned around and he talked with her. She whispered to him while winking her eye. "Go back. Go back home," she said softly.

The boy was provoked and he called out as he left the church, "You can stay there a-winking and a-blinking, but them sheep are butting all the dumplings out of the pot."

Zackie Knox
As told to Genevieve W. Chandler, WPA field worker.
Murrells Inlet, South Carolina 1937.

ᦶ ᦷ

Tricky Rabbit and Buh Gator

Buh Rabbit used to go down to the river in his day. He call Buh Gator out. They talk. Buh Rabbit say, "Buh Gator, I have so much trouble I ain't know what to do."

Buh Gator say, "Trouble, Buh Rabbit?"

"Yes, trouble."

"I ain't know what trouble is. I ain't never have no trouble," Buh Gator say.

"You ain't never had no trouble? Well, I'm coming down here tomorrow and I'll show you what trouble is."

Buh Gator say, "All right."

You see, Buh Gator be happy. He wanta know what trouble was.

Next day Buh Rabbit come down. He say, "Well, Buh Gator, you go off and lay in the broom-grass field. You go to sleep and you wake up and you see trouble."

Buh Gator gone off to the broom-grass field. Went to sleep. Buh Rabbit get coals outa fireplace. Gone all around field, a-setting fire. He say, "Trouble, Buh Gator."

Buh Gator raise he head and see no fire but he see smoke. And he raise up again, and fire be on him. He make way through the fire and jump in the river. Fire burn and crack he back up. That is why Buh Gator's back is cracked up till today.

Zackie Knox
As told to Genevieve W. Chandler, WPA field worker.
Murrells Inlet, South Carolina May 2, 1937.

Before and After Freedom

My Father and the Whiskey

You see, before Freedom we plant rice at Brookgreen Plantation. My father had the barn key. He was kinder the boss man. Sometimes when he went to the woods at nighttime, he took me with him. I held the torch for him to see by. My father took some of the rice from the barn to Georgetown and sold it and bought liquor. Boss find out about my father. He figured a way to make him forget about the liquor.

Each Saturday, each family's rations for the next week were piled up in the barn. There was a pile of rations for each member of the family. When my father's name was called, he went to the rations and started to pick them up. The boss broke a liquor jug and held the broken glass toward my father to indicate he would cut his hand to pieces. Every time my father reached for a pile of rations, the boss jabbed the broken glass toward him to discourage him from wanting whiskey. My father took the broken jug and got no rations for about a year. Boss was a mean man.

Ben Horry
As told to Genevieve W. Chandler, WPA field worker.
Murrells Inlet, South Carolina 1937.

Buh Rabbit and Buh Guinea

Buh Rabbit and Buh Guinea like to work together. One day they meet a cow. They thief the cow and kill her and clean out all the entrails. They leave her there. Buh Rabbit say, "Oh, Buh Guinea, See that red fire yonder? Get a piece of that fire and we'll cook a piece of cow and eat her." Buh Rabbit show Buh Guinea the red sun.

Buh Guinea fly and fly. A day and a night and he couldn't get to the red fire. He turn back. When he get back he see no cow. He see Buh Rabbit.

Buh Rabbit say, "I went off in the bush and wink my eye and I come back and all the cow done sink in the ground. Ain't nothing but the tail out. Now you and me can pull the tail and get the cow." Buh Rabbit knew he done carry all the cow meat home and give it to the little rabbits.

Buh Rabbit and Buh Guinea pull and pull. The tail pop out.

Buh Rabbit say, "Let us dig."

They dig and they dig till they come to some water. They didn't find the cow.

Buh Guinea say, "I hungry. Better roast this tail."

Buh Guinea roast the tail and eat a piece and fall back and say he dead.

Buh Rabbit think the tail and the other meat that he done give to the little rabbits musta been pizen. He didn't want the little rabbits to eat pizen. He run home and fetch all the meat back where he was.

Buh Guinea say, "Buh Rabbit, you fool. But you don't fool me. We gwine share this meat even." Buh Guinea jump up and share it out even and start home.

The man who owned the cow see Buh Guinea and Buh Rabbit. Start to shout.

Buh Guinea and Buh Rabbit drop the meat in the bushes and run.

When the man gone, Buh Rabbit and Buh Guinea come back and get meat. They gone home.

Cato Singleton
As told to Genevieve W. Chandler, WPA field worker.
Murrells Inlet, South Carolina 1937.

The Balloon

A young German name of Count Zeppelin invite me to go up in his balloon. When we reach a certain height, I saw the Blue and Grey armies meet at a point just outside Charleston and engage in battle. Zeppelin was attached to the Federal forces. He was the guest of a general who commanded a battery on Morris Island, across the Ashley River from the city. He came to the United States when he was about twenty-five years old. His first balloon trip was at Fort Snelling, near St. Paul, Minnesota. That started him to thinking 'bout the construction of a balloon which could be navigated. I made the balloon flight. My eyes were good. Any object I saw, I knew what it was. We went up on the other side of Beaufain Street and came down on Citadel Green.

I was born in Limestone, Virginia. Tony was my father. He was the carriage driver. He wore his tall hat and fine livery. He was a musician and played the violin on the old Ninety-Six Road. The white people had parties. Oh, the beautifulest ladies. They wore long dresses then and had long hair, the beautifulest. My father, Daddy Tony they call him, play the songs of that day, before the War of 1861. One of them went: Would have been married forty years ago, if it hadn't been for Cotton-eyed Joe. My father played the violin.

Before and After Freedom

I been sold when I was ten-years old; not really sold, but sold on a paper that say if he didn't take care of me, I would come back. Then I came to Maussa Cherry, at Orangeburg. Maussa had plenty of money.

Richard Mack
As told to J.O.C. Tiedeman, WPA field worker.
Charleston, South Carolina.

Parson Glennie

In 1829 Francis Marion Weston, a wealthy Georgetown County rice planter, brought Alexander Glennie from Scotland to tutor his son, Plowden C.J. Weston. After Glennie had taught Plowden everything he believed he was capable of teaching, he accompanied the student to England and enrolled him at Harrow. The people of All Saints Parish realized how effective Glennie had been with the planter families and their slaves. All Saints was without a rector at the time and a call went across the sea to Glennie to return and study for holy orders. Glennie came to South Carolina and met with the people of the parish. He explained that he was dismayed that the children of the slaves were being given no religious training. "They are not learning the Catechism," he admonished. Glennie suggested that the planters build chapels on their property for the specific use of the slave children. He would visit each plantation once each month, he promised, and on the Sundays he could not visit, he expected the mistress of the plantation to fill in for him. Glennie was hired.

After the children's program was set in motion, Bishop Philander Chase, from Philadelphia, visited the Lowcountry. After he returned home he wrote an article for a national journal saying that the black children of the coast of South Carolina knew more of Christianity than the white people in other parts of the country.

South Carolina slave narratives are filled with references to Parson Glennie. The one told by Mariah Heyward goes like this:

I was birthed on November 5, 1855. Parson Glennie lived at the Rectory and did a wonderful job teaching and preaching to slaves as well as white. He preached at all the chapels, including beautiful Saint Mary's at Hagley Plantation. The baptismal font from that chapel is now at Camden Episcopal Church and a stained glass window is in the Prince George Winyah Episcopal Church at Georgetown. Parson Glennie came once a month to Sunnyside. He read, sang and prayed. Told us to obey Miss Minna. Miss Minna tell us to be good or she would tell Parson Glennie. We people at Sunnyside summered at Magnolia Island. Rowed to Bull Creek once a month to the plantation chapel. Ten miles or more. Go to All Saints services too. Four bent rowmen took us over. They were the best rowmen of all. And they could sing.

Mariah Heyward
As told to Genevieve W. Chandler, WPA field worker.
Murrells Inlet, South Carolina 1937.

Maussa was a Little Boy

When I was just a little girl, staying in Beaufort at Missus' house, polishing brass andirons and scrubbing her floors, she say, "Janie, take this note to Mr. Willcox's Wholesale Store on Bay Street, and fetch me back the package the clerk gives you."

I take the note. Mr. Willcox read it. He give me a little package to take back to Missus. She open it and say, "Go upstairs, Miss!"

It was a raw cowhide strap about two feet long, and she commence to pour it on me, all the way upstairs. I didn't know what she was whipping me about.

"You can't say, 'Maussa Henry,' can you?"

"Yes'm, I can say 'Maussa Henry'."

Maussa Henry be just a little boy 'bout three-or four-years old. Come 'bout halfway up to me. Want me to call a baby 'Maussa!' I regret ever going to Beaufort.

Mama and four of us chillun were sold to Maussa Robert Oswald, in Beaufort. Pa belong to another man. Mama was an unusual good washer and ironer. White folks been saying, "Wonder who it is that's making the clothes look so good." One day the Missus call her to the house to read her something from a letter. Letter say Papa done marry another woman. Mama wipe her eyes with her apron, first one eye then the other.

We stay in Beaufort, but I have to call a baby 'Maussa.

Rebecca Jane Grant
As told to Phoebe Faucette, WPA field worker.
Beaufort, South Carolina.

Before and After Freedom

❧

That Would Be the Difference

I, Thomas, was born on Pee Dee Plantation in 1850. I was a uniformed footman a-sitting up proud on the box of the carriage. The Civil War change my life but not my loyalty. I offer to do Missus' garden work free of charge. "But, Thomas, I'll pay you now." "No, Missus. I want you to buy me a rake and a hoe, suitable for gardening, not too big, but strong and useful. I don't know how much they will cost."

She give me some money and say for me to go buy what I need.

When I finish the task, I hand her the change. I say, "Missus, when I was coming back with the hoe and rake, I meet a man. He hail me, 'What you doing with that hoe and rake?'

"My young Missus send me to buy 'em," I say.

"You got any change?"

"A little."

"What you gwine do with the change?"

"Return to my young Missus."

"You fool. Don't return that," he say.

I gave Missus the change and say, "Now if you ain't been my Missus, that would be the difference.

Thomas
As told to Martha Pinckney, WPA field worker.
Charleston, South Carolina.

❧

'Mancipation

When war come, I been minding cow for Maussa. My father been Moses Mitchell and my mother been Tyra Mitchell. We belong to John Chaplin and live on Woodlawn Plantation on Lady's Island. Maussa Chaplin had seven plantations. He lived at Brickyard Plantation in winter and in Beaufort in summer. Fifteen slaves live on Woodlawn.

Maussa had nine chillun. Six boys in Rebel Army. That Wednesday in November when first gun shoot to Bay Point, I thought it been thunder rolling but there ain't no clouds. My mother say, "Son, that ain't no thunder. The Yankees have come to give you your freedom." I been so glad. I jump up and down and run.

When 'mancipation come, my father get job as carpenter. He bought ten acres of land on Lady's Island.

Sam Mitchell
As told to Chlotilde Martin, WPA field worker.
Beaufort, South Carolina.

∾ ∾

Buh Rabbit Tricks Buh Gator

Once 'pon a time, Buh Gator been in the pond. Buh Rabbit went to the pond with a harp and start to play. Lingly Station, piggy-pig-piggy, bang-a-lang, Lingly Station bang-a-lang.

Buh Gator rise up out of pond and say, "Who that playing that pretty tune?"

Buh Rabbit say, "All right, Buh Gator, you come on out and dance to this tune. Go through my legs fast and come back through my legs slow-like."

When Buh Gator come back through the legs, Buh Rabbit strike his head with a hammer. Buh Gator roll over and jump in the pond. Buh Rabbit gone.

Next morning Buh Rabbit come back dressed as a squirrel. "Lingly Station, piggy-pig-piggy, bang-a-lang."

Buh Gator rise up out of pond and say, "Good morning, Buh Squirrel. Buh Rabbit was here yesterday a-singing that same tune, and when I come out, he say, 'Go through my legs fast and come back slow.' When I come back, he knock me with the hammer on my head. If he been knock me on my knot, he been kill me, but he hit me on my head."

Buh Squirrel say, "Yeah, Buh Rabbit always play that dirty trick. Come on now and dance for me. I won't do you so."

When Buh Gator went through his legs and came back, Buh Squirrel strike him on the knot and kill him. He take Buh Gator's tusk off his head and carry it and give it to the governor.

As told to Chlotilde Martin, WPA field worker.
Beaufort, South Carolina.

∾ ∾

21

Buh Wolf

Once 'pon a time there was a little girl a-walking in the woods. She see some flowers. She break the flowers. Just then she see Buh Wolf.

Buh Wolf say, "Lil girl, sing a song for me lessen I eat you up."

Little girl sang, "Ta! Ta! Ta! Ta!"

Little girl got down the road. Buh Wolf see her again. Buh Wolf say, "Lil girl, sing that song again lessen I eat you up."

Little girl sing, "Ta! Ta! Ta! Ta!"

Little girl go home and tell her mama she had to sing the song "Ta! Ta! Ta! Ta!" lessen the wolf eat her up.

And that's the end of that story. Little girl's mama not let her go to the woods again.

As told to C.S. Murray, WPA District Supervisor.
Charleston, South Carolina.

⌒⌒

Brookgreen Snakes

What you think about the elder a-talking about snakes? What you think about it? You think a man trusts himself to go in the cypress hollow with the rattlesnakes? The elder's story went like this: On the Rutledge plantation a man wouldn't take no beating. He found a large, hollow cypress tree what been rottened out many years. Gone in. Lie down to sleep. He wake up fore day. Feel something a-crawling over him. Sound like a mother crow a-crowing like a game chicken. Smell him. Crawled over him and crawled out. The Revents say in that story that a man go in a cypress tree and twelve monster-snakes crawl over him. Couldn't move. Iffen he move, a snake will strike. J. Ward Flagg, our maussa, have a big old stable. Stable high as a tree. Big Jersey bull gone in there a-eating straw. Big rattlesnake pop the bull. Bull fall dead right there in the barn.

Ben Horry
As told to Genevieve W. Chandler, WPA field worker.
Brookgreen, South Carolina.

⌒⌒

Caesar's Cure

About 10:00 pm on the evening of August 17, 1967, I left my Charlotte, North Carolina home and walked to the garage to check on some lamps my husband had made for our beach cottage. I had no trouble seeing my way across the porch and yard, but when I stepped into the doorway of the garage building, it was as dark as midnight. Suddenly, I felt something puncture the skin on my left leg from the knee to the ankle it seemed. I turned on the overhead-light and there by my foot, coiled about three or four times, was a shiny snake. I had been bitten many times at close range. I did what anyone would do—let out a blood-curdling scream. A neighbor heard me, ran over and asked another neighbor to take me to Charlotte Memorial Hospital. There I was told they would have to obtain the snake in order to answer two questions: Was the snake of a poisonous species and had it expelled all of its venom into my leg. After a call was made to my home, the snake was killed and taken to the hospital to be examined. The serpent was a copperhead and had expelled all of its venom into my leg. My treatment consisted of the maximum dosage of horse serum. After several weeks, I was fully recovered and the swelling in my leg and foot had gone away. I began to wonder what people did many years ago when horse serum was not available. Fortunately for the people of South Carolina, an enslaved African named Caesar perfected a formula for such a medical emergency.

Caesar became particularly famed for his cure, which was successfully used by Henry Middleton, the founder of Middleton Place Gardens near Charleston. In 1750, the legislature ordered Caesar's prescription published for the benefit of the public, and the *Charleston Journal*, which published it, found its copies exhausted by the demand. The ancient script of the records reveal:

The Cure for Poison: Take the leaves of plantain and wild hoar hound, golden rod roots and lye. Boil them together in two quarts of water and strain it. Of this concoction let the patient take one-third part three mornings from which if he finds any relief it may be confirmed he is perfectly recovered.

Caesar was given his freedom in honor of his discovery.

Nancy Rhyne.
Columbia, South Carolina.

Beauregard's Method of Eating Fish

When Beauregard ate fish, he wouldn't pick a bone out. He just worked them out of the corner of his mouth. He learned to eat fish in that manner from a very old woman who lived in a cabin on the Waccamaw River in Georgetown County. Beauregard stood at her door one day and watched as she ate a plate of catfish. Beauregard drew as close to the old woman as he could. As he watched over her shoulder, he discovered she was eating rice along with the fish. The fish had not been properly cleaned and the bones went into the woman's mouth and thoroughly chewed. From the left-hand corner of her mouth there poured a steady stream of half-chewed bones.

As Beauregard stood there, a kitten, lured by the delicious smell of the fish, approached stealthily and finally reaching the old lady's knee, jumped up and sniffed with appreciation of a good odor. Putting down her spoon and with arms akimbo, Auntie measured the cat with her eyes. She announced deliberately, "Kitteny, if you wants to face your God this day, put your nose in my bittle [vittles]."

Ben Horry
As told to Genevieve W. Chandler, WPA field worker.
Murrells Inlet, South Carolina 1936.

No One Died on Edingsville Beach

Eberson Murray returned to his island home after the Civil War. He and his family had spent the war years in Newberry. Years after the Murray family returned to the coastal area, Eberson's son, Chalmers, who was employed as a field worker for the WPA, interviewed his father and wrote the following account:

"Upon our return to the plantation from Newberry County, we found our twenty-room home on the coast in ashes. Every tree had been cut down for firewood. Grand oaks they were. The government returned the plantation to us. The land without capital was of little use.

Later on, conditions took a turn for the better. Money could be borrowed. Sea Island cotton brought on the market an enormous price of from one to two dollars a pound. Then the caterpillars descended and destroyed every cotton crop before it reached maturity. We knew nothing about fighting the worms with poison. The result was inevitable. Loans could not be paid back and mortgages were foreclosed. It was years before we could fight back."

Eberson Murray had returned to his home at Edingsville Beach, near Edisto Island. He enjoyed writing romance stories. Some of his tales were published in The *Youth's Companion* and other magazines. He served also as the Edisto Island correspondent for the *Charleston News and Courier*. He was a sixth generation Edisto islander. His favorite meal consisted of hot hominy and fried shrimp. His favorite view was of Edingsville Beach.

The topography of Edingsville Beach, which is no longer in existence, was much the same as that of other barrier islands. Behind the big white sand dunes was a thick impenetrable jungle of cassina, china berry vines, honeysuckles and yucca. Houses were shaded by oaks and laurel.

Dwellings were spaced far apart and stood in two long rows, one row overlooking the ocean and the other the marshland and creeks. Children fished, ate raw palmetto cabbage (the heart of a palmetto tree), made bonfires and played in the surf.

Lessons at the village school were taught by Miss Mary Lee, a daughter of the Reverend States Lee, pastor of the island's Presbyterian Church for over fifty years. Reverend William Johnson was rector of the Episcopal Church. He hauled firewood in a little wagon on which he rigged a sail. When the wind was right, he would hoist his sail with his firewood aboard, and skim along at a high rate of speed. Life on Edingsville was ideal. Health conditions were all that could be desired. No one died on Edingsville.

C.S. Murray, WPA District Supervisor.
Edisto Island, South Carolina 1936.

 ‿ ‿

The Beautiful Lady on the Ship

In the early days of Georgetown's history, the ships from England landed at the foot of Screven Street, behind the old city hall, with its picturesque tower. One day a shipload of passengers from England made port in Georgetown. The passengers were a group of dissenters, fleeing persecution in England. Among them was a lovely young girl of high-born parentage. She had embraced the faith of the dissenters from the Orthodox Church of England and thereby brought upon her young head the wrath of her noble father, who was too close to the king to make it comfortable for him to have a member of his family a dissenter. She was, therefore, disinherited. In desperation, she joined a party of dissenters who were making ready to sail to America and freedom.

Before and After Freedom

After weeks of weary sailing, the little ship docked in Georgetown. The lovely young girl was on deck. A strange sight met her eyes. Come to meet the boat was a motley array of merchants. On the outer-fringe of the crowd, mounted on a handsome black horse, was a well-groomed man in his early thirties. He owned a lucrative property some twenty miles inland and was a confirmed bachelor.

After the other passengers had left the ship, the young woman stood alone at the rail, gazing out forlornly at the strange and alien gathering. Inborn courage, a heritage of her noble lineage, came to her assistance. She stood proud and tearless and asked in a clear voice, "Is there anyone here who will give a home to a lonely girl who is willing to work?"

A dramatic silence followed. Then, from the outer edge of the group, a horseman pushed his way nearer to the landing. Overcome by her beauty and the sweetness of her voice, the confused bachelor replied by asking her to come ashore. He dismounted and before helping her to his horse he said he would gladly give her a home and the tenderest of care upon one condition: That was that she would become his wife.

After looking into his fine grey eyes and seeing there the promise of future happiness, she agreed and the two rode away together to found one of the substantial and respected families of Georgetown County.

As told to Genevieve W. Chandler, WPA field worker.
Murrells Inlet, South Carolina 1936.

ↄ ↄ

The Tar Baby

There was a rabbit and a billy goat and the land was very dry. Not a drop of rain had fallen from April to July. The animals had no water. Didn't know how to get water.

Buh Rabbit tell 'em, "Oh, man, I wake up in the morning and get my dew."

Billy goat tell 'em, "No, man. We try that. We don't get no water from dew."

Buh Rabbit tell 'em, "You ain't quick enough."

Billy goat watch that night and Buh Rabbit gone down to his well just a-whistling. Billy goat see Buh Rabbit's well and he go and tell all the animals. "Buh Rabbit get his water from his well." They decide to set up a tar baby. They make a pretty tar baby and set 'em near Buh Rabbit's well. Buh Rabbit gone down there and see the tar baby.

"Hey, dere," Buh Rabbit say. "Hey, dere, pretty gal."

Tar baby say nothing.

"You better talk to me! If I slap you one time with my right hand, I'll break your jaw."

Tar baby ain't say nothing.

Buh Rabbit slap his right hand and it stick to tar baby.

Buh Rabbit say, "If I slap you again, my left hand will knock you one-sided. One time I slap a gal and I had to pay twenty dollars for it."

Tar baby ain't say nothing.

Buh Rabbbit slap 'em with his left hand. His left hand stuck to tar baby.

"If I kick you with this foot, I'll bust your belly open." After Buh Rabbit done kick tar baby his left foot been stuck. He kick tar-baby with his right foot and it stuck.

"I know one thing," Buh Rabbit say. "I got a belly. If I butt you with my belly, I'll bust you open."

He butt him with belly. Belly stuck to tar baby.

"I got a head and teeth. If I butt you with this head and teeth, you won't do nothing but die."

He knock 'em with he head and bite 'em with he teeth and all of that stick.

Buh Rabbit can't do nothing now.

Billy goat gone. All the animals come. They tell Buh Rabbit, "We got you now!"

The Billy goat and all the animals take Buh Rabbit from the tar baby and carry 'em home. And they didn't know what they would do with the tar baby. They wouldn't touch 'em.

Cato Singleton

As told to Genevieve W. Chandler, WPA field worker.

Murrells Inlet, South Carolina.

∾ ∽

Mom Cinchy

Missus, you say that old man looks like an angel? You can't always tell, Missus. Nothing can be told by the outside look. That old man. Look at his wife. There is Mom Cinchy.

Take Mom Cinchy: She works in the rain and heat. She works in season and out of season. She plants the rice seed. She jumps on the rice. She cleans 'em. She hoe the big rice fields three times in the boiling sun. Helps hoist the water gate for the free-flow of the river water. The first flow of the river water is the sprout flow. After the seed has sprouted, the water is sent back to the river. Then they have the harvest flow. That fulls 'em out and takes away the insects. Water sent back to river. Mom Cinchy makes a full crop. Harvest time comes and she stands there with them chillun and waves her arms and hollers for to scare away the rice birds what'll clean up the crop if they not kept away.

Before and After Freedom

Harvest comes. Mom Cinchy take hook and bend she buckles [knee joints] *and cut 'em with her two hands. She bundles them. She stacks them. Then time comes to tote 'em down to the flat boat and flat 'em to the barnyard. Mom Cinchy is the one what takes the pole in hand and poles that boat to the home landing. She totes 'em to the ox cart. She trail the ox cart through them deep, hot sand uphill and downhill to the thrashing yard. Then she thrash 'em. She handle flail same like man.*

Mom Cinchy climb the high step on that platform and holds that big winnowing basket over she head. The chaff fly! She winnow them same like a strong man. Mom Cinchy have the strong arm. She clean 'em and when everything been taken out she sack 'em. Yes, suh, she sack 'em and drag 'em into the barn.

And what happen? Mom Cinchy's onliest body child took down. Chill and fevers grab holt on her boy, Laban. Mother answer the call. Mom Cinchy nurse Laban and cool the fever with sea-sage tea. She come over Waccamaw. And half the rice gone. She ain't say nothing. But she know ain't no human being doesn't do that 'cept her own man, Gabe. That same old man what you think look so good and got the angel name. Mom Cinchy ain't say nothing. She suffer and she ain't crack her mouth.

Mom Cinchy have she little partridge and she cash 'em in to pay the Revents and clothes for her "turning out." All members of the Heaven's Gate Methodist Church must dress in white. Gloves. Hat and dress. She wear the high-top shoe for to keep her foots dry. And she needs her tobacco. She like her pipe. And Mom Cinchy have to pay her lodge dues so she can be put away right.

Mariah Heyward
As told to Genevieve W. Chandler, WPA field worker.
Murrells Inlet, South Carolina 1937.

ॐ ॐ

Freedom on Sandy Island

Sandy Island is not a barrier island. It is surrounded by the Waccamaw and Pee Dee Rivers, and today it is accessible only by boat. The island has been populated largely by the same family groups for more than a century. Most of the surnames of the families on Sandy Island are the same as those of the plantation owners a hundred-and fifty-years ago. Sandy Island, its hills of white sand and forests, surrounded by abandoned rice fields and rivers, still bears the names of the old plantations. A woman said to someone from the mainland, "I live at Montarena Plantation." Many of the old Sandy Islanders, such as Gabe Lance, lie in the cemetery, but their stories live on, especially the tales of the day when 'mancipation came to Sandy Island.

"*Peace. Great peace,*" *said Gabe Lance.* "*I can remember when the Yankee boats come to Montarena. Guns. Boats. About ten o'clock in the morning. Soldier all muster out and scatter all over the island. You know that causeway? Come over that two by two, gun on shoulder glisten 'gainst the sun. Blue coats, blue pants, hat all blue. Tell us we be free. 'Mancipation! They come back to landing about five o'clock. Have hog, geese, duck. They broke in barn. Stole rations from poor people. My grandfather was the driver, slave driver. Name of Nelson. Maussa was Frank Herriott. Maussa gone in swamp. Hid in woods. My grandfather take old Miss Sally, Missus Sally Herriott, on account of she couldn't walk with rheumatism. Grandfather took old Missus Sally on his back and hid 'em in the woods where Maussa been. Yankee stay but that one day. Ravage all over us island. All goat, hog, chicken, duck, geese, all the animal but the cow been take on the Yankee gunboat. They broke in Maussa big rice barn.*

Some of my people ran away from Sandy Island. Go clean to The Oaks at the seashore and Magnolia Beach and take rowboat and gone out and join with the Yankee. Them crowd never did come back.

Gabe Lance
As told to Genevieve W. Chandler, WPA field worker.
Murrells Inlet, South Carolina.

⚭

The Spirits of Hagley

It was in the summer of 1918 that I underwent an experience that was destined to change my life. I didn't have a shadow of a doubt that spirits make an earthly appearance now and then.

I never remember having any fear of supernatural beings and like most people, I thought that spirits were merely products of an over-wrought imagination. The things I saw that summer demonstrated very plainly that I was wrong.

At the time, I was engaged in carrying passengers between Pawleys Island and the ferry landing at Hagley Plantation, on the Waccamaw Neck. I used a large automobile and made the trip several times a day. Often, a party of young people who were working in Georgetown would hire a gasoline launch after the ferry had made its last trip, and I would meet them at Hagley at 11:00 pm.

Reaching the ferry landing about a quarter to eleven, I thought I would stretch out on a piece of old canvas on the wharf and get a little rest before the boat arrived from the city. The moon was shining brightly, flooding the landscape with a soft glow and every object was

plainly visible. The scene was a peaceful one, and a few minutes after I had made myself comfortable I fell asleep.

The dream that came to me that night was so vivid that I can remember every detail. I was standing with a crowd of people in front of the little church and it seemed that we were waiting for the bride and groom to emerge from the front door. Everyone was dressed in clothing of the Civil War period. I got the impression that peace had just been declared. Suddenly the bridal party appeared on the porch. The bride was a striking brunette, and the groom handsome blond.

The crowd rushed for the porch. A man dressed in a Confederate uniform dashed up to the clearing astride a horse that evidently had been running for hours. The figure dismounted and ran towards the place where the bride and groom were standing. When he reached the couple, the bride uttered a little cry and said, "It is too late. I have just married another." She said she waited three years and believed he had been killed in battle. The stranger said to the groom, "Well, I will fade out of the picture. It is the best solution." The groom answered, "No, if anyone must fade, I will be that one."

The soldier made for the wharf, followed by the bride and groom. When he reached the end of the pier, he jumped in and disappeared. Without a moment's hesitation, the bride followed him, and then the groom.

I rubbed my eyes and looked about the pier. The church and the people had disappeared. I got up and turned around and noticed a couple standing nearby. They resembled the bride and groom.

I believed someone was playing a trick on me. I said politely, "Who are you? If you are waiting to go to Pawleys I have an automobile nearby."

The couple turned around and walked slowly away. I had scarcely collected my wits when a motorboat arrived. The passengers I was waiting for were on board. "Hello," someone said. I tried to hide my agitation. "You look as though you just saw a ghost," he added. I told him I had seen two of them but we must get on our way to the beach.

Later on in the season, on another moonlight night, I made my customary trip to Hagley to meet a special boat, which was due at midnight. The vessel arrived and my guests comfortably seated in my car. As I sped toward the seashore, two figures stepped into the road. One was a brunette bride and the other a blond groom. I stopped the car so suddenly that my guests were thrown about. I collected myself and drove on.

When we reached the beach, the girl beside me turned to me and said, "Eugene, I know why you stopped so suddenly. A man and a woman were in the road."

I told her I had seen them and barely missed hitting them.

Eugene F. LaBruce
As told to C.S. Murray, WPA District Supervisor.
Edisto Island, South Carolina.

⤳ ⤳

Sassafras Tea

During the Civil War our ports were blockaded by the Yankees and we Charlestonians were cut off from the world. We were used to the luxuries that came into the harbor on ships and it came as a shock that we could not receive the pleasurable items we thought we couldn't live without. The ships had brought us riches, wares and merchandise almost beyond our comprehension. Blue and purple shawls from Europe warmed our arms; crystal and silver bowls, goblets and plates brought splendor to our homes; oil and balm for pleasure and medicinal purposes soothed our skin; ivory from foreign coasts adorned our tables, white wool warmed us; choicest spices flavored our food; and multicolored apparel and garments embroidered in gold dressed us for the balls. All of it was gone. Yankee ships guarded the harbor.

We had to make the most of what we had at home except for the slender ships that ran the blockade and got some supplies in that manner. Make do, became a slogan. Sister Liz's macaroons were made of peanuts instead of almonds, which could not be had in war times. Jelly was made of pigs' feet, and it was delicious. Confederate cake, rich with huckleberries and whatever dried fruit was to be had and sweetened with sugar from the molasses barrel was a favorite dessert. We sat together at night and had potatoes and milk and sassafras tea. Oh, the sassafras tea. It was grand. One who has never had to depend on sassafras tea does not know how satisfying it can be.

Mary Huger Gibbs Ball
As told to Irma L. Bennett, WPA field worker.
Charleston, South Carolina.

⤳ ⤳

Sarah

Everything and everybody was astir at an early hour at The Wedge *and breakfast, a bountiful meal, often kept the family at table for two hours.*

Immediately after breakfast there was the ritual of morning prayer which Sarah always looked forward to, not so much for the spiritual uplift but for the privilege it offered of studying with vivid imagination and much awe the titles of the hundred or more books in the massive bookcase which stood almost in front of the spot where her chair was placed. One particular red and gold volume fascinated her so irresistibly that she was once punished severely for spelling out the title Dawees on Children, *quite audibly in her father's reading of the Scripture.*

Before and After Freedom

The young Irish governess was entrusted with the guiding of the minds of Sarah and her sisters. Sarah leaned her ABCs out of the Bible. She would spend hours lying flat on her stomach in front of the blazing-log fire, with the big book spread out on the floor before her. Girls were taught to handle a needle at an early age. When Sarah was only eight she could sew the finest seam and hand-tuck the daintiest pantaloon cuffs. She made a handsome sampler when we was nine and was expert at piecing quilts. Sarah later attended a select girls' school in Charleston.

During long winter evenings, while her father read aloud, and her mother and sisters were busy at sewing and embroidery, Sarah's job was to pick little seeds from cotton, piled in a big basket placed beside her chair.

When bedtime came, Sarah's body servant, Pink, would undress, bathe and tuck her in, making sure that the foot warmer was in place and with a "Goodnight Missie" that left her with pleasant dreams.

Sarah Lucas
As told to Irma L. Bennett, WPA field worker.
Charleston, South Carolina December 12, 1937.

ᑫ ᑲ

Mr. Allston's Boyhood

My father's childhood was spent at Mt. Moriah Plantation, on the Santee River. By 1850 he would insist on getting up and being dressed at the crack of dawn to ride with my grandfather on his customary rounds of the plantation. Breakfast was a bountiful meal. Curds, made in a heart-shaped mold, covered with nutmeg and cream, clabber, sweet wafers, shrimp, hominy and corn cakes were on my father's plate. It was my grandfather's custom to ask a blessing in a very low tone.

My father's pony was named March, because he was born in that month. My father, who was a little boy, caught, bridled and saddled him, assisted by Cumsy, whose name was Tecumseh, my father's faithful body servant. Cumsy trailed along behind my father on his marsh-tacky pony named December. My father first used a gun when he was nine-years old. It was a cut-down breechloader.

My grandfather imported a tutor from Germany for the children. Religious training was stressed. No sport of any kind interfered with the family prayer hours, morning, noon and evening-tide. All the servants of the household were present. There were many outbursts of "Yes, Lord," and "Amen."

Mrs. E.L. Johnson
As told to Irma L. Bennett, WPA field worker.
Charleston, South Carolina 1939.

ᦕ ᦖ

Riding the Sheep

Our whole family was a horse-loving family and learned to ride at an early age. I was taught to ride a black sheep when I was four-years old. We were living at the old Bentham house, at the corner of Smith and Vanderhorst streets in Charleston. It was a domain. The grounds ran through to Calhoun Street. In the garden was a grape arbor about fifty-feet long, with all sorts of grapes on it. Twelve fig trees provided figs for us.

The black sheep had a way of darting into the rose bushes or under the arbor and, fearing that I would get my face scratched, my father taught me to ride facing the tail. My brothers faced forward. When the sheep darted under the arbor, my brothers caught hold of the upper branches of the grape vines and swung there, but I was too little to reach them.

The next year, when I was five-years old, we were playing in the garden with an old horse that our father had given us, taking turns riding her. My father brought a friend out to see the horse. The gentleman asked my father if he was not afraid I would get hurt. "Oh, no," he said. "She is quite an equestrienne herself."

My father learned to ride on his fourth birthday. Moses was his body servant. Moses would pull the horse's head down and hold it while my father stepped up on the ears of the horse and hauled himself up by the mane. He would sit there on the neck, facing the rear, until Moses lifted him and turned him around to face the horse's head.

Alice Barnwell Ewbank
As told to Jessie A. Butler, WPA field worker.
Charleston, South Carolina.

ᦕ ᦖ

After We Moved to Summerville

There were many sportsmen in Summerville. If a deer was shot, it was cut into six pieces. The man who shot it was given first selection of the parts. The loin and haunches were considered the choice pieces. The men were surprised that my father often asked for a shoulder. He was particularly fond of the part known as the back-strap, the large muscle which runs from the back of the neck down the back. When this is cut into rings and properly broiled it is tender and juicy.

Alice Barnwell Ewbank
As told to Jessie A. Butler, WPA field worker.
Charleston, South Carolina.

~ ~

Buh Cooter and Buh Deer

Buh Cooter tell Buh Deer, "Bet you can't beat me to the mile post."

Buh Deer say, "Bet I can."

Now Buh Cooter have a great nation of people. When they come out and start to run, Buh Deer strike out and leave Buh Cooter behind. Buh Cooter see he was first to the mile post.

Buh Deer go to the next mile post. He ask, "Who due at next mile post?"

Buh Deer say, "Well, let me put out to the next station." He run 'til he get to the last mile post. When he get there, Buh Cooter say, "Here I is."

Buh Cooter beat that race.

As told to Chlotilde Martin, WPA field worker.
Beaufort, South Carolina.

~ ~

A Faithful Servant

My father belonged to Judge Prioleau and was trained to wait on the table from the time he was a boy. Judge Prioleau liked Hoppin' John. The master told his servant, my father, to heat up the Hoppin' John. The master said, "Heat it." But my father thought he said, "Eat it." After my father ate the Hoppin' John, the master commenced to whip my father. The Maussa's daughter stopped that. She explained that my father did not understand what the Judge had said. The Judge forgave my father.

In later years, when Maussa was paralyzed, my father was his attendant. He wouldn't leave Maussa. Before Maussa died, he was laid on a couch. My father slipped himself under the couch and slept there, near his master. After Maussa died, he was fixed up nice-like and laid out on the same couch. My father lay under the couch, to feel close to his Maussa in death.

Susan Nelson
As told to Martha Pinckney, WPA field worker.
Charleston, South Carolina.

೨ ৩

The Circumnavigator

I was born in Charleston when the city belonged to England. When I was nine-years old a famous man named Lord Anson came to visit my father. Lord Anson was called "The Circumnavigator." That word means "one who sails around the world."

Besides ships and sailing, Lord Anson loved gambling more than anything else. He gambled every chance he got. He even gambled with sailors on his own ship. Lord Anson usually won. He gambled with my father, who had to give him all of his property in Charleston known as Ansonborough. Oh, how very sad that was. My father often walked through the streets of Ansonborough, clutching his wrists and looking grim. He probably was thinking, "Some day I'll buy my property back again."

I went to school and studied French, Hebrew, Algebra and what were called "the learned languages." I studied hard and went to Europe on a tour. When I came back to America I went to work for a rich merchant in Philadelphia.

By-and-by I came back to Charleston and became a rich merchant. I did not build a mansion and live in the manner of the blue bloods. I bought back the land that my father had lost to Lord Anson and lived all of my life in a little cottage known as Anson House.

Christopher Gadsden
As told to Rose D. Workman, WPA field worker.
Charleston, South Carolina 1937.

೨ ৩

The Last Rice Crop

The last commercial crop of rice in North Carolina, South Carolina and Georgia was planted at Laurel Spring and Rose Hill plantations. These are adjoining plantations, which I, Theodore D. Ravenel, then owned. They were situated on the Combahee River near Green Pond, South Carolina. Four hundred acres were then under cultivation, which was a small portion of the usual amount. In the fall of that year, 16,000 bushels were harvested and shipped to market through Green Pond. The price received for 43 ¾ pounds to the bushel was $1.15.

Once I was asked if I could cite instances in which rice was used for barter. "Hell, no," I replied. "A rice planter would rather have starved than stoop to barter with rice as the commodity."

I went on to state that the planter took care of the rice culture entirely, leaving the selling to a broker who made the returns to the planter.

When I became owner of the plantation, I planted 700 acres in rice and continued to produce until 1926. E. F. Hutton purchased at least eight plantations from me. Hutton's total property comprised some 10,000 acres in Colleton County. [E. F. Hutton's wife at that time was the former Marjorie Merriweather Post. She was known as the richest woman in the world. Mar-A-Lago the home she built in Palm Beach, is now owned by Donald Trump and considered as one of the most magnificent estates in North and South America. Mrs. Hutton spent $20 million on Mar-A-Lago during its construction from 1920 to 1928.]

Theodore Ravenel
As told to Gardiner H. Walker, WPA field worker.
Charleston, South Carolina 1939.
Additional information from Nancy Rhyne.

What Judge Samuel H. Wilds Said to John Slater on the Murder of His Own Slave

John Slater!

You have been convicted by a jury of your country for the willful murder of your own slave; and I am sorry to say, the short, impressive, uncontradicted testimony, on which that conviction was formed, leaves but little room to doubt its propriety...

You caused your unoffending, unresisting slave to be bound hand and foot, and by a refinement in cruelty, compelled his companion, perhaps the friend of his heart, to chop his head with an axe, and to cast his body, yet convulsing with the agonies of death, into the water, and this deed you dared to perpetrate in the very harbor of Charleston, within a few yards of the shore, unblushingly in the face of open day.

Had your murderous arm been trained against your equal, whom the laws of self-defense protect, your crime would not have been without precedent and would have seemed less horrid...

In proceeding to pass the sentence which the law provides for your offense, I confess I never felt more forcibly the want of power to make respected the laws of my country, whose minister I am.

Samuel H. Wilds
As told to Mrs. Harry Rogers, WPA field worker.
Blenheim, South Carolina 1936.

∾ ∿

Judge Wilds's Famous Sentence

The duty, which yet remains to be performed towards you, of all others to me the most awful and distressing, it is my misfortune to be obliged to perform alone. The laws of one common country have commissioned me to announce to you your doom. I hold your death warrant in my hand. Death, the great destroyer of man, is terrible even in its mildest forms, though we behold its destructive ravages spread wide around us; though we behold the rich, the poor, the old, the young, the virtuous, the vicious, fall indiscriminately before its deadly scythe, and feel our own fate inevitable, still we cannot contemplate its frightful approaches but with the most fearful apprehensions.

The awful uncertainties of a future state, the untried vicissitudes of the unknown world, whence none who have gone have ever returned, appall the strongest hearts; and like cowards, we groan under the pressure of life's many ills, fearful to draw aside the veil which hides the future from us. But, though death be always dreadful, it is not always equally so to yield lives to Him who gave them; to wait the dread moment on our beds of sickness, surrounded by those we love, whose affectionate concern, whose sympathizing tears soften the anguish of expiring nature; to die for our native land, to guard its honor on the field of danger, and meet the grim tyrant at the cannon's mouth, though not enough to make him welcome, robs him of half his terrors.

But unfortunately for you these are consolations, which will not support you in your approaching doom. The life which God hath given you, you have yourself wickedly destroyed; the tender love, the sympathetic tear which would have cleaved to your departing spirit, and winged it for its flight, you have banished your public disgrace, to pine in hopeless solitude over your untimely fate; and to offend the justice of that country, for whose honor to have died would have been heroic, you fall a victim.

Hung up between the heavens and the earth, Heaven's oldest, greatest cause stamped on the deed you have done; no friendly voice to bid a long farewell; no friendly hand to close your eyes in death, you will exhibit an awful but instructive spectacle to the world and prove that the arm of avenging justice is swift to overtake him who sheds his brother's blood.

I need not remind you, for you cannot have forgotten the circumstances, which led to this fatal catastrophe. Your hands yet smoke with the blood of murder, and nature's newly made grave makes an impressive appeal to your memory. Your drunkenness but aggravates your crime; the diabolical fury which drove you on to perpetuate this fatal deed, seems not to have had any exciting cause; and the insidious, cowardly maneuver in which you made the attack, the deadly weapon which you wielded, and your unmanly perseverance in inflicting the deepest injuries on an adversary, who had not made the slightest resistance; nay, who was even unable to raise his hand against you, argue a most savage temperament of soul, a heart black with malevolence, and more than ordinate depraved.

Before and After Freedom

You have had a fair and impartial trial by juries of your choice, in the selection of whom even your caprice has been tenderly indulged; you have had the benefit of able counsel, whose manly address to the understanding, whose eloquent appeals to the heart, must have saved you, if even a doubt guilt could have been excited; but alas, it has all been in vain; you have been pronounced guilty of the horrid crime of murder, for which you die unpitied.

I will be hardly generous to remind you, for it can now only aggravate your distress, of the many strong inducements which you had for a different conduct. Living in a land of light and liberty, where every right is securely protected, every virtuous exertion liberally regarded, in the vigor of health and prime of manhood, and surrounded by all the means of honest enjoyment, life was surely worth preserving. You have—but my heart sickens at the thought—a wife, who tenderly loves you; you are a father of children, who look to you for bread, for them at least you ought to have lived. Cruel, thoughtless man, what have you done?

But if the laws of your country, and your country's God, if the love of life, and its varied enjoyments; if the distress and disgrace of a family you love; were unable to withhold your murderous arm; yet, believe me when I assure you, a reason yet more powerful than all, ought to have made you pause. You have a mortal soul at stake, and have by this fatal deed, to the manifold transgressions, added a mountain of guilt.

Your days on earth are numbered. The sword of death, which hang uplifted over the frail thread of your existence, ready to drop, will quickly cut it in twain, and those who have known you, will know you no more. But though you feel the fatal stroke, hope not in it to find a termination of your woes. It will be the mere prelude to another trial, awfully terrific. Again you will be arraigned at the bar of justice, and the black record of a thousand crimes spread in your view. Again you must raise your trembling hand, but before a judge whose penetrating eyes will spy the secret corners of your soul, whose power is fearful indeed.

Again you will be confronted with witnesses—and, horrible thought, the bleeding, murdered Mathis, probably dragged from the howling regions of despair, will appear in the number; should you again be found guilty, your doom will be interminable woe. Let me conjure you by every tie which yet has a hold on your heart, to devote the scanty remnant of your days to serious preparation for your approaching doom. Strive importunately, I beseech you, to secure that Advocate, whose merits are all powerful, whose service alone can save you, for in the exhaustless fountain of redeeming grace, even the foul stain of murder may be washed clean.

The sentence of the court is, that you be now carried from hence to the place from whence you came and that on the last Friday in May next, between the hours of eleven and forenoon in the afternoon, you be carried to the place of public execution, in the District of Union, there to be hanged by the neck until your body be dead, and may the Almighty God have mercy on your soul.

Samuel H. Wilds, a judge of much renown, was born in Marlborough District of South Carolina, in 1775, and died at the early age of thirty-five years.

Mrs. Harry Rogers, WPA field worker.
Blenheim, South Carolina 1936.

A Woman on Her Feet

Oh man, if I was to tell you the truth this afternoon, Missus, Hampton Plantation was heaven to me and everybody else. Because the big old flat, the boat you call the flat, come from the place you call Blake. That was where Dr. Archibald Rutledge's father, Henry Rutledge, got his first wife, Dolly Blake. And Colonel Rutledge brought my great-grandmother from Blake. [Sue pronounced Blake as if it were Bleck.] *My grandmother and my father and mother were slavery-time people. The Yankees came down and freed everybody. That's why I love the Yankees. I never met a Yankee I didn't like.*

The ballroom ceiling is two-stories high. At Christmas it took big old tree to fit in there. You walk from the dining room to the living room. And from the living room you go into the ballroom. Oh man, them Christmastime had more hallelujah. Dr. Rutledge's mother had them bring in that big tree, and she had plenty of sugar, coffee, and everything that people had need of in that day and time. That was the biggest time, 'cause we had the gingham dress and things.

We had such good pig. And we hang the hams up and there was always ham for the table. And duck, and turkey. The ham was from the yard, you know. Not this season's ham; last season's ham. I spend all day long in that little kitchen behind the big house. It take a full day for me to cook the ham and slice it, and put it on the tray and carry it to the pantry of the big house.

Oh, golly, it just fills me up when I think about how wonderful me ole Missus was. Oh, she was a woman on her feet. I marry Prince Alston in nineteen aught five [1905] *and after I begin to bear my children, why me ole Missus took my children like they were hers. And she would be there when she know that baby about to come. That was Missus Margaret Hamilton Seabrook Rutledge. That was Archibald's mother, not Archibald's wife.*

The slavery time was the roughest time they ever had. 'Specially the no-manners people. That's why I feel everybody should have manners and principle. You should have that. If you don't have a nickel in your pocket or a penny, you should have that. No I tell them I don't care how old I get, I can be up or down, but do for heaven's sake, give me credit for having manners

and principle. My grandmother and my mother teach me, my father, my grandpeople, all my people teach me manners.

My great-grandmother Lydia she always sit down and tell us what it was like—the day freedom came. She said when the Yankee come they rode the horses through the house. They rode them from the front to the back and then back to the front and down the steps.

We had old sideboard. They tell me when the Yankees come the old man Alston—the one who was real Hampton people—he worked for the Horry people, you know, they tell me he took that sideboard and he hide 'em in the swamp they call Dark Mouth. That's where the Colonel tell him to put 'em, you know. And they tell me when they come, the Yankees didn't do nothing too bad to Hampton.

The Yankee people used to come to Hampton when it was Colonel Rutledge's place every week. Every week! Oooo and I loved them so. Oh, yes ma'am. The people from the North, I really loved them. And my grandmother and my great-grandmother told me the day that the Yankees come and free Hampton and tell Dr. Rutledge's father, now you know, Henry, he was the colonel in the war, they said he was so good to his people that all the colored people wanted to go to Hampton. Archie Rutledge's father and his grandfather be so good to the Rutledge people that everybody wanted to go to Hampton. Oh, Missus, you talk about rice, meat, turkey, duck, chicken, egg, you could pick up eggs in the basket, have basket and pick 'em up, they lay all around everywhere. That was the best place.

They have parties at Hampton. Some Hampton people go to work at six o'clock in the morning, and some who had a real job got to go back at six o'clock in the evening. That party be right there in that ballroom. Dance? The white people dance!

It was something, Missus, at the Hampton place, and I was right there. Yes, ma'am, I was right there!

I bake them ole cake for the weddings at Hampton. I wish you could have seen it, Missus. Seen it like it was way back in them days.

I go to church at Hampton, and I give a shout. I shout! Who can stop me? If it didn't be for the Lord, I wouldn't still be here to talk to you. All the things I ask God Almighty up there for, He takes care of. He ain't coming while you call Him, but don't you give up calling! He's an answering man! That's why, to tell you the truth, I may as well tell you the truth about it, white people, and I'm a Negro person, I love white people. According to my experience and what I always been used to, I'm not going to leave that. Me great-grand, me grand, me children, have manners and principle. If you don't have nothing else, have that.

Me ole Missus's preacher was named Moses. He was a bishop, and he would come to Hampton twice a year and preach. I tell you, Missus, I cry when I think of the Colonel and me ole Missus. I just miss them so. I still miss them so much. Me ole Missus died at the place they call Fairfield, not far from Hampton. And the day Dr. Archibald Rutledge died, that was a broken-hearted day.

I might live to be a hundred. But I don't mind what I see as much as what I do. I know I love the Lord. He told me if I kept what He gave me I would be safe. I had an aunt who lived to be one hundred and twenty-eight. Her name was Fanny German.

Missus, I could count on me mug of tea at four o'clock in the morning just as sure as the sun would rise. Hampton Plantation manor house was filled with love. You can have a mansion, and it is not a home. You can have a shack and it is not a home. I cooked at Hampton house. I cleaned it up. I answered the door, made up the beds, took care of the children. After the death of me ole Missus and Colonel Henry Rutledge, and after their children left home, I slept there. Oh I took care of it because it was my home.

Sue Colleton Alston was the daughter of emancipated slaves. When she died in 1983, she was believed to be 110 years old.

As told to Nancy Rhyne.
Columbia, South Carolina.

∞ ∽

The Bronze Tablet

On a fine, substantial, old-brick gatepost at 80 Alexander Street in Charleston, owned by Mr. E.B. Refo, there is a handsome bronze tablet bearing the following inscription:

Near this spot once stood The Liberty Tree Where Colonial Independence Was first advocated by Christopher Gadsden A.D. 1766 and where, ten years later The Declaration of Independence was first heard and applauded by South Carolinians.

C.S. Murray, WPA District Supervisor.

∞ ∽

The Denmark Vesey Insurrection

My great-grandfather was a son of Robert Nesbitt and he tell us 'bout the Vesey uprising as his Daddy tell it to him. He say one hundred and thirty-one slaves, including his father were brought to trial as a result of the secret plan of Vesey and his friends, to take over the City of Charleston and kill off the white folks.

Denmark Vesey came to Charleston from the West Indies with his owner, Captain Vesey, a rich, white importer from Charleston. For fifteen-to twenty-years Vesey was a faithful slave. 'Bout 1800,

Before and After Freedom

when Denmark Vesey was thirty-three years old, he won $1,500 in a lottery. With this money he bought his freedom from Captain Vesey for $600. He was very careful what he did with the rest of the money, always keeping it where it would be safe, and he worked every day at the trade of carpentry. He spoke French and English good and became respected by other slaves and white folks. He was sowing the seeds of discontent amongst Charleston Negroes and in other districts. He was sly. White folks didn't 'suspicion him. They believed he was a right smart man.

Denmark Vesey held meetings at his house at midnight and he would swear his members to secrecy. My great-grandfather attended a meeting one night. He and Vesey were friends. But my great-grandfather never took no part in the planning, 'cause he tried all the time to show Vesey he was riding for a fall and was playing with dynamite. He tell Vesey he be taking too big a dare and the plan was too dangerous and he didn't want to take a wrong step in that.

After my great-grandfather tell him this, Vesey smile and stand up and tell 'em, "Take care. Don't mention this plan to no waiting slave who gets old coats and extra clothes and things."

The meeting broke up and the slaves scattered out to their quarters and sho' as you is born, it was one of these same waiting men that tattle the secret to the masters. The masters have their own meeting and spread the news 'bout the Vesey rebellion. The revolt was squelched and the leaders were tried before a special court, in which Robert Y. Hayne appeared to be rising to distinction.

The case against Vesey gets its start. Judge calls order in the court. All the Charleston maussas be a-sitting right there.

Vesey take stand as his own lawyer. Others of the rebels were hanged.

The court found that the Negro leaders planned to kill all the white folks in the saddle. My great-grandfather say he never see so much tumult in his born days as there was when the Vesey crowd was hanged, twenty-eight found not guilty and acquitted and the rest deported from South Carolina.

Great-grandfather say the loyalty of the slave to his master be so deep under the skin of the slaves that it was even stronger than the dream of freedom. He say there were three kinds of slaves, the slave who was just plain bad, the slave who would rather suffer the ills than take the chance of going to others he did not know and the ones a-waiting for the lone chance of making a getaway.

My great-grandfather was the leader in the prisoners who were acquitted in the Vesey case. He was a family man, big property owner in Charleston. My own grandfather was pretty well-fixed but generally speaking, Jordan Road has been pretty stumpy for the rest of us. I tell my chillun to get all the schooling they can, trust in God and they won't go for wrong.

Israel Nesbitt
As told to Stiles M. Scruggs, WPA field worker.

The Stono Insurrection

In 1739 there was an uprising at Stono, near Johns Island, a few miles southwest of Charles Town. On the 9th of September, 1739 a number of men held in bondage assembled at Stono and began their movement by breaking open a store, killing two young men who guarded the warehouse and plundering it with guns and ammunition. They chose one of their number as captain, and marched in the direction of Florida with colors flying and drums beating. On their way they entered the house of a Mr. Godfrey, murdered him, his wife and children, took all the arms in the house setting fire to it, and proceeded to Jacksonboro. In their march they plundered and burned every house, killed the white people and compelled others to join them. Lieutenant Governor Bull, who was on his way to Charles Town, probably from Beaufort, observing this body of armed men, rode out of his way and avoided them. He crossed over to Johns Island into Charles Town with the news.

It was Sunday and the alarm was given at church. By a law of the province, all persons were required to carry arms to church. Mr. Golightly led the men of the church and engaged in a fight with the slaves, several miles from Charles Town.

For fifteen miles the insurgents had spread desolation through all the plantations on their way. Having found some rum in some houses and having drunk freely of it, they halted and began to sing and dance. During these rejoicings, the Militia came up and took positions to prevent escape, then advancing and killing some. The remainder of the men dispersed and fled to the woods. Many ran back to the plantations to which they belonged, but the greater part were taken and tried. Some of those who had been compelled to join were pardoned; the leaders suffered death.

Twenty-one whites and forty-four Blacks lost their lives in this insurrection.

Apart from the Spanish propaganda the widespread of the rebellion made it evident that there must have been some substantial cause for this feeling of hatred evinced by so many slaves toward their masters. They were human, and only a spark was needed to set such heated tinder into flame.

As told to C.S. Murray, WPA District Supervisor.

ᘜᘛ

Blockade Running During the Civil War

A haze against the starlight moved across the dark expanse of water in the direction of Fort Sumter. For flashes of a second it seemed to take form, then began to blur and, like beautiful music, it faded and was gone.

Before and After Freedom

As yet the lookouts of the Federal squadron of blockaders stationed in Charleston harbor and the waters outside had noticed nothing. Blockade runners did not ordinarily choose starlight nights on which to make port under the very guns of the monitors. It was safer to run in under cover of darkness or under the blanket of a fog. Even a raging storm offered fewer hazards than a night like this.

The phantom, driven forward by the wind, moved slowly. Suddenly from the obscurity arose what seemed to be a jack-o-lantern gone to sea. In reality it was a vagrant spark which had escaped through the damper in the smokestack of the Hattie, one of the most fearless of the blockade runners that plied the waters around Charleston.

Almost automatically there was a sudden flare of rockets from the ironside, Housatonic, which was standing so close that those above deck on the Hattie had heard the order. The first rocket announced to the other Federal ships the presence of a blockade runner. Those following were pointed in the direction of her course.

A rapid fire of cannon from the entire fleet responded. Discovered, the Hattie was given full speed ahead and steered straight for the channel. She was directed by two friendly beams flashed upon her signal from Fort Sumter. The fleet pursued, belching fire, smoke and shell. The Hattie's captain stood on the bridge, his coat sleeves hitched up almost to his armpits, a sign of intense excitement with him. Other than this he was as cool as glass.

For ten minutes the Hattie ran a gauntlet of shot-and-shell from the gunboats, which steamed straight ahead. They stopped only short of within pistol range of Fort Sumter, then so battered to pieces that the monitors threw caution to the wind when a prize was at stake.

The Hattie, elusive as the sea breeze, skirted on untouched. Then came the peril. Just below Sumter, in the narrowest part of the channel, she ran upon two barge loads of men stationed on picket. Except for her speed she would have been boarded. The volleys fired after her cut three fingers off the hand of the pilot holding the wheel, but the Hattie had hung up a record for tripe not exceeded by any other vessel engaged in the business. The real peril was yet to come.

She swung into the harbor and was soon headed up the Ashley River to the West Point Mill wharves. Charleston was being bombarded. It was no longer possible to dock in the Cooper River and there dispose of her cargo to agents as she had once done.

Aboard were munitions of which the Confederacy was in dismal need. In addition there were wines; brandies; medical supplies for the hospitals; needles; even ribbons and, perhaps, a bit of lace; a baby basket purchased especially by the pilot for his expected heir; a few toys and shoes that would not fit the feet of the Southern women who would be so fortunate as to get them.

These were hastily unloaded. In their place the little boat was soon stacked to the gunwales with cotton destined for Nassau there to be traded chiefly for munitions.

No time was lost. The Hattie was in as much danger lying at the wharf as she would be outside. It was clear that the city must soon fall. Shells from the Swamp Angel and other long-range guns had burst as far uptown as Charlotte Street and 101 Saint Philip Street. In the lower part of the city shops and homes had been abandoned. Few other than the boys from the

Signal Corps who kept a lookout from St. Michael's steeple, the chief target, remained there. The foxes and rabbits to which this part of the city had been left had to creep about as cautiously as the blockade runners.

As soon as her cargo was made up, the Hattie *was ready for the outward voyage. The Confederacy was in need. The cause was at stake. It did not matter to her gallant captain that the sentinels off Fort Sumter had that day counted twenty-six Federal blockaders including the formidable* Housatonic *and the* Potapsco.

Just before midnight, twenty-four hours after her arrival in port, the little craft headed out over a smooth sea and under a sky studded with stars. She was a small vessel, Clyde, *built with powerful engines. Painted a lead color she sat low in the water. She had telescoping smokestacks, which could be lowered at will almost level with the deck. As most of the blockade runners, she was a side-wheeler. Likewise her wheels were provided with feathering paddles in order that the revolutions should make the least possible noise. Around the guards of the wheels were fastened securely curtains of stout canvas. These, heavily weighted with chain at the bottom, hung deep down into the water so that neither the phosphorescence nor the white froth stirred by the paddles could be seen by the fleet. She was burning a boarded supply of anthracite coal so as to have as little smoke and spark as possible until she had passed through the blockade squadron.*

Before the Hattie *swung out of the Ashley River, every light was put out except the light in the binnacle on the bridge and the lights actually needed in the engine and fire rooms. Those were closely guarded lest the least ray escape. That in the binnacle had over it a long funnel-shaped arrangement made of canvas and strengthened and kept in place with hoops. At the upper end it reached the eye of the man at the wheel who saw the compass through a hole about one and one-half inches in diameter.*

She moved with absolute quietness relieved only by commands given by a positive voice in undertone, "Port; hard a-port; steady; hard a-starboard."

Proceeding at half speed offshore from Sullivan's Island, past Drunken Dick Shoal, she picked her way until she had cleared the channel. Then began the perilous crossing of the bar, which had to be negotiated before the fall of the tide. Eyes and care of those above deck were strained for outlying pickets before the blockaders outside should be sighted. In the stillness the rustle of winds when a duck was startled was disturbing. Even the casual flight of a gull brought concern.

A messenger aboard, his dispatch case in a heavy canvas bag heavily weighted with iron, stood ready to consign the private papers of the Confederacy to the deep if necessary.

At length the bar was crossed in safety. With every heaving of the load the soundings became deeper. Then the fleet loomed black and ominous under the starlight. The Hattie *crept silently and safely past as though she bore as a figurehead the left hind foot of a graveyard rabbit.*

As she passed the last monitor a blast of rockets shot above her like an umbrella. A picket boat had given the alarm. A flaming echo of other rockets came from the Hattie. *These were sent in*

a contrary direction, which served to mislead the lookouts on the fleet. There was a confusion of lights as the fleet responded with signals and searchlights.

Seizing the advantage the captain of the Hattie *ordered an eight-point change of course. Going to the speaking tube, he called down to the chief engineer, "Give her hell, Mr. Jones."*

The engineer ordered the dampers off the funnels. Black smoke and flame poured from them. The vessel trembled from stern to stern as she skidded swiftly before the pursuers.

But the blockaders began to loom up closer one after the other. Shells burst over and around the Hattie. *One glanced the bridge but did no damage. Another exploded among the bales of cotton and set fire to them. Powerful pumps put out the blaze.*

The watchers on the bridge were not pleased. The captain spoke to the engineer again, "Mr. Jones. We must do better."

"Sho' will do better, Sir," was the response.

In a few seconds some members of the crew were at work cutting some of the bands from the cotton bales while others knocked in the head of a barrel of turpentine. The cotton was saturated with turpentine and then fed to the furnaces.

Flames five-feet high poured from the funnels. The Hattie *sprang over the water with the fleetness of a hunted deer. The fire under the boilers was so intense that the pitch in the seams of the deck above the boilers began to sizzle so that it was necessary to keep a constant stream of water spraying over the area. So terrific were the vibrations that the two pet cats on board were terrified. They went creeping about with eyes distended and tails dragging upon the deck as they sought in vain for a quiet place to rest. Yet Charleston was the principal center of the blockade on the south Atlantic coastline. The purchasing officer of the Confederacy was stationed here. Likewise there was a concentration of enemy fighting vessels at this port.*

Two voyages were enough to pay for the craft and still net a handsome profit. Successful blockade runners rolled in wealth. There were others not so lucky. Failure meant imprisonment, loss of fame and fortune, or else consignment to Davy Jones' locker at the bottom of the sea.

Because of the great amount of money needed, few vessels were privately owned or captained by the owner. As a usual thing, syndicates were formed abroad and at home to engage in the trade. Those who shared in the enterprise in an economic way risked their worldly fortune to the same extent that those who ventured at sea risked their lives.

A blockade of Southern ports was proclaimed by President Lincoln on April 27, 1861. For a period it was called the "paper blockade" since the Federal Navy at that time was too weak to watch three thousand miles of coastline.

For nearly two years the Federal patrol was a joke. The Confederacy, whose credit was excellent abroad, offered an inducement to swift merchantmen to dump large cargoes of munitions of war at Southern ports and take in return cotton so necessary to the looms of Europe.

During this period the blockade runners were almost exclusively officered by the English and Scotch. In 1864 the stringency of the blockade became extreme. Most of the profit was taken out

of privateering. Then only patricianism induced men to risk all. No one but a Confederate would take one chance out of twenty and consider the odds in his favor.

Nearly all the officers during the last two years were Confederates. It is an interesting fact that no blockade runner commanded by an officer in the Confederate Navy was ever captured.

Many of the blockade runners left Nassau and Bermuda "on moons" so as to arrive at a Southern port under cover of darkness with their precious "hardware" and other manufactured goods. Many plied with the precision of regular packet steamers until the last southern port had fallen.

Charleston became a blockade center in the beginning because of her commercial importance but she remained so until the end because she offered peculiar advantages to blockade runners and, due to the natural layout of her fortifications, was capable of defense almost to the last against attacks by sea.

The blockade runners that came into Charleston Harbor had the additional protection offered by naval boats known as torpedoes. The Confederate Congress legalized torpedoes in October of 1862, establishing a Torpedo Bureau and training a special corps of officers and men. The torpedoes had been used previously by the Russians in the Crimea though none of the enemy vessels were destroyed by them.

After their introduction into Charleston harbor these little boats were known as Davids, taking their name after the first one of their class. The first David was built as a private enterprise of Theodore Stoney of Charleston. With a volunteer crew of four the David succeeded in permanently disabling the Ironsides and then reaching the city in safety. Other of these little torpedo steamers were responsible for the sinking of the Patapsco, the Tecumseh, and some of the smaller vessels of the blockading squadron.

The Housatonic met her fate in Charleston waters, the victim of the first submarine known officially as the Hunley but popularly called the Fish Boat. This boat with a crew of eight had a bad way of diving unexpectedly nose-on into the muddy bottom and sticking. Five crews gave their lives successively but the fifth accomplished the sinking of the USS Housatonic. From the sinking of this ship in 1864 until 1914 no other submarine succeeded in sinking a hostile war vessel. The names of the daring men who served on the Hunley are listed in a bronze tablet in White Point Garden at the foot of Meeting Street in Charleston. The history of that ship and the vessel itself can be seen in Charleston.

After the nature of the naval warfare and the need for guns and supplies became so desperate, the blockading business began to pay enormously when successful. This condition lasted only about eighteen months. The men who made money were those who held on to their salaries and profited after each voyage from the sale of a bale or two of cotton. The pay of the captain was usually $5,000 a round trip or $10,000 a month. Others of the crew were paid in proportion. Before the war $150 a month was the usual pay of captain of a merchantman.

The names of many of the vessels represented their captains or sponsors. Among those about Charleston were the Chicora, Banshee, Let Her Rip, Southern Cross, Vulture,

Falcon, Phantom, Siren, Venus, Don, Robert E. Lee, Hattie, Margaret and Jessie, *and* Everain O. Fox.

The Robert E. Lee *was one of the best of the blockade runners. She was once the* Giraffe, *a mail boat plying between Belfast, Ireland and Glasgow, Scotland. The Confederate Navy Department bought her for $150,000 and changed her name to the* Robert E. Lee. *She ran the blockade twenty-one times carrying over 7,000 bales of cotton valued at over $2 million. This money was spent abroad by Confederate agents for arms, ammunitions, hospital supplies and much needed goods. The blockaders supplied the very life blood to the Confederate Army. Without them the essentials of warfare would have been denied a cotton kingdom.*

Margaret Wilkinson
As told to C.S. Murray, WPA District Supervisor.
Edisto Island, South Carolina.

Vanderbilt Buys the Last Alston Plantation

Early in the second half of the 18th century the men of the Alston family of St. John's Berkley looked about for better land for the production of indigo and rice. They spotted the Waccamaw River section of Georgetown County. Between then and 1800 many plantations were carved from the jungle-like forests that bordered the rivers, including Fairfield, Brookgreen, The Oaks, Crowfield, Clifton, Rose Hill, Pleasant Hill and smaller tracts on the peninsular south of the Horry County line. The Allstons raised indigo and rice. Through the Allston mansions, in Georgetown County and their Charleston homes, passed many a noble. It has been written that servants, at Clifton Plantation, William Alston's plantation on the Waccamaw River, wore uniforms of green plush, faced in red and trimmed in silver, with silver buttons. In 1851 Mrs. Charles Alston, whose husband Charles, a son of William Alston of Clifton, owned Fairfield Plantation, was preparing for an upcoming ball at her home at 21 East Battery in Charleston and made a list of supplies that began:

18 dozn plates; 14 dozn knives; 28 dozn spoons; 6 dozn wine glasses; as many Champaign glasses as can be collected; 4 wild turkeys; 4 hams 2 for sandwiches and 2 for the supper tables;

8 patés; 60 partridges; 6 pr of pheasants; 6 pr canvas-back ducks; 5 pr of our wild ducks; 8 Charlotte Russes; 4 pyramids 2 of crystallized fruit & 2 of Cocoanut; 4 orange baskets; 4 Italian creams; an immense quantity of bonbons; 7 dozn cocoanut rings; 7 dozn Kiss cakes; 7 dozn macaroons; 4 moulds of jelly 4 of Bavarian cream; 3 dollars worth of celery and lettuce; 10 quarts of oysters; 4 cakes of chocolate; coffee; 4 small black cakes.

All Allston men were members of the Jockey Club. Their thoroughbreds regularly raced at Charleston's Washington Race Course.

William Alston changed the spelling of his patronymic name to its original English spelling with one "l" and began the line of one "L" Alstons. He commissioned Jonathan Lucas in 1790 to build mills powered by tidewater to pound his rice, and this was the beginning of an extensive rice culture.

By 1900 hardly a title to an Alston plantation was still in the Alston name. Some had been sold to President Roosevelt's friend and Morgan partner, Bernard Mannes Baruch; Brookgreen to Archer M. Huntington and others to Isaac Emerson to form his giant plantation and game preserve, Arcadia. At Emerson's death in 1931 he left Arcadia to his grandson, George Vanderbilt.

One day George Vanderbilt's agents went to Fairfield's Elizabeth Deas Alston with an offer to buy. Vanderbilt's Arcadia Plantation surrounded Fairfield. Fairfield was sold to George Vanderbilt for $40,000. Gone from Waccamaw was the last holding of the family that for 200 years was its most influential.

When George Vanderbilt died in the early 1960s, he left Arcadia Plantation, including Fairfield, to his daughter, Mrs. Lucille Vanderbilt Pate. The author of this book interviewed Mrs. Pate several times in Pate's elegant drawing room at Arcadia Plantation. One day Mrs. Pate said, "Mr. father was able to buy Fairfield. That was something my grandfather had wanted more than anything but they would not sell. My father bought Fairfield and that completed the group. Up into that time it just sat there in the midst of all the other plantations. The property didn't seem complete until my father bought Fairfield."

Dromgoole Ham, WPA field worker.
Florence, South Carolina 1938.
Additional information on the 21 East Battery Home from Nancy Rhyne.

Before and After Freedom

De Flagg Storm

I reckon they calls the storm that 'cause it done wipe out most of the Flagg family. Thirteen head of 'em gone on Friday the thirteenth of October 1893. That's where they were. Right there on Magnolia Beach. The Flagg women, men and chillun were there on the island at high tide.

Me and the old woman had been called for court. The old colonel was the magistrate and he call a court to try a man who had an argument with his wife. My old woman was called for a witness. We start for home. The court been over. The rain come in so fast my old woman had to ford the end of the salt creek. There weren't no causeway, and you had to do what you had to do when the tide came in. We were in the ox cart. The tide ain't never run out that day. High all day. Never saw oyster rock or sand bar on that day. We came to the salt creek and the storm was rushing in. Behind us, across the sand beach, the sea been lighted up. He been lighted same like lantern light the house. He looked same like fire. We were anxious for to get across that salt creek. That sea made us think about judgment and hell. Sea look like he been on fire. As we hit the creek, the creek been light up. Sea and creek been shining. We urge our ox. Ox won't move. The tide was coming in fast. We were in that boggy place. Ole woman pull and I push, and us two been a-praying. The moss was a-flying from trees like bird. The wind talked and moaned same like human. The plat eye been frequent. Every which-er-way the tree been groaning. Rotten limbs falling all around. We hear the sounds from the Will Go Church. The sound of the prayers reach we. They were all a-praying. Good and bad was united. People go down in prayer. Ask God for to speak to the wind and waves. Ask Him to calm the elements. Beg Him for to say, "Peace be still." When the young men are inspired, they preach, they testify, they pleads with God, they shout. They don't crave no vittles, they don't eat, they fall in trance, same like dead human. After the elements calmed down, they had to be toted off.

What happen over on Magnolia Beach? Miss Georgia [Mrs. Arthur Flagg, Sr.] gone. She and her husband been holding onto limb of cedar tree. House done gone to sea. Miss Georgia's husband, Dr. Flagg, he see she lose her hold on the tree, and he turn loose and take her in embrace and they go to sea together. The storm lick 'em out. The young doctor, Doctor J. Ward Flagg, he see father and mother a-floating by. Mom Adeline been floating by, and the young doctor grab and say "Hold on." The swells begin to roll out. The water go back to the deep.

The people on the hill? They take to the woods and make a run for higher ground. Much corpse been lying in the marsh. Cow been in the live oak. Carcass hang high. The buzzard been a-feasting. We sing a song 'bout the storm. I most forget it, but it go like this: The wind so high. He blow so hard. We just don't know what for to do. Then we recognize it be the wonderful power of God. Two hundred bodies come a-floating by. We ain't know just what for to do. Then we recognize in it, the wonderful power of God.

Mr. and Mrs. Cato Singleton
As told to Genevieve W. Chandler, WPA field worker.
Murrells Inlet, South Carolina 1937.

50

∽ ⌒

The Horse Racing Aristocracy

The year 1734 may be fixed as the first year of turf in the history of South Carolina. The earliest existing record of any public running appeared in the *South Carolina Gazette* on February 1, 1734. The prize was a saddle and bridle valued at twenty pounds sterling. In 1735 the York Course was laid out at the Quarter House. In 1754 the New Market course was all the rage, and the meets were in February or March. Prizes were a silver bowl, tankard or other piece of plate valued at around one hundred pounds currency. The New Market Course continued in use until 1792 when the South Carolina Jockey Club moved to the Washington Race Course [near the entrance to the Citadel today]. It sponsored racing until 1899.

Among the original proprietors and owners of the Washington Course were General Charles Cotesworth Pinckney, General William Washington, William Alston, General Wade Hampton, William Moultrie, Edward Fenwick and General John McPherson. The South Carolina Jockey Club was the outstanding organization of its kind in the state and second to none in national prestige. The races were held purely for the sport of matching horses—"Your blood is from Virginia; mine is fancy blood from Europe."

The first great importer and breeder of the thoroughbred horse in South Carolina was Sir Edward Fenwick (1720–1775) founder of the Johns Island Stud. He imported *Brutus*, a grandson of the Godolphin Arabian. He continued to import until there were eight stallions and six mares. In 1755 Fenwick imported a stallion *Matchless*, the last surviving son of the Godolphin Arabian. Fenwick's foundation stock was Chickasaw. Only on his daughters did Fenwick render more praise and favor, and it was one of his daughters who suffered one of the most tragic romances in South Carolina history.

Fenwick's fairest daughter committed the unforgivable sin of falling in love with her father's head groom. After eloping on one of Sir Edward's swiftest thoroughbreds, they were delayed at the Stono Ferry, where they were overtaken by members of the family, headed by the girl's enraged father. Then and there, her husband-to-be was tried by a mock court and convicted as a horse thief. Sir Edward's daughter was pulled from the horse but her lover remained in the saddle. The horse was led under an oak tree and a noose was placed around his neck. When her father handed the girl his riding crop and ordered her to strike the horse on the backside she refused, realizing the horse would leap ahead and her fiancé would hang from the tree limb. Her supplications were disregarded. Sir Edward insisted his daughter use the riding crop, and the young man was hanged upon an oak tree before her eyes. Her mind never recovered from the shock, and tradition says her spirit still walks the grounds of Fenwick Hall on Johns Island.

Margaret Wilkinson, WPA field worker.
C.S. Murray, WPA District Supervisor.

The Criminals Who Were Never Hanged

Coosawhatchie, a tiny village on US 17, five miles from Ridgeland, in Jasper County, was an Indian village known as the "Refuge of the Coosaws." The Indian name has remained until this day. Coosawhatchie was also the scene of a Revolutionary battle between the forces of General Augustine Provost and Lieutenant Colonel John Laurens, in which Colonel Laurens was wounded. It was at this little village that General Robert E. Lee established headquarters when he assumed command of the Confederate Military Department of South Carolina during the War Between the States.

A sketch of the village was written by William John Grayson, poet and writer, born in Beaufort in 1788, in his book *The Life of J. L. Petrigru* . Entitled "A Unique Jail," it is as follows: Coosahwatchie, at that time the judicial capital of Beaufort District, lies on the road that leads from Charleston to Savannah and always was so well situated for catching bilious fever [malaria fever] as never to miss it. It was hardly habitable in summer, to live in the village for two consecutive summers was almost impossible for a white man and few attempted it. One exception was Mr. Bassilue, who kept a shop and furnished board and lodging for lawyers and clients in term-time. He was able to live with country fever in all its varieties, as conjurers in Bengal handle venomous serpents without harm or damage. He must have been anointed in infancy with some patent drug of mysterious efficacy. The alligator in the neighboring creek was not safer than he. To every white male but himself, a summer in Coosawhatchie was death. It was unnecessary to try a criminal there charged with a capital offense. All that was required was to put him in jail in May to wait his trial at the November court. The state paid for a coffin and saved the expenses of trial and execution. At night the jailor thought it unnecessary to remain in the jail. He locked his doors and went away to some healthier place until morning, confident that his prisoners had neither strength nor spirit to escape.

At last the lawyers became dissatisfied. They loved fair play, as well as fees, and desired to see the rogues brought to justice in the regular way with a chance for their lives, such as the assistance of a lawyers always affords them. The general jail delivery brought about by fever prevented the thief from being duly hanged and the counsel from receiving his retainer. The culprit escaped the halter through the climate, not the bar.

Finally the old laws passed into antiquity and normality rushed in to take its place. When someone was indicted for a crime, that person was tried in a court of law and the defendant had proper counsel. A jury sat in the box and if the defendant escaped the halter it was through the bar, not the climate.

From the WPA field workers' files, author unknown.

∿ ∽

Money on the Grave

Friends from Davidson, North Carolina told me they were walking in the Citizens Cemetery, an ancient cemetery in Beaufort, reading inscriptions on stones, when they happened upon a grave that was completely covered in quarters, dimes, nickels and pennies. The mound of money was several inches high. Confused about such a discovery, the visitors left immediately and located a city office, where they described what they had seen. They said the people who worked for the city claimed they knew nothing of such a mound of money and advised the visitors not to violate the grave in any manner.

Three days later, my husband Sid and I had a couple of free days and visited Beaufort, the most charming of towns and surely one of the quaintest. Coming into town on US 21, it was clear why we had never noticed the Citizens Cemetery. Immediately across the street was the National Cemetery, which naturally draws attention. Sid pulled off the road at the Citizens Cemetery and parked under a tree.

I took my stance on the northern side of the burial ground and Sid went to the southern side. We agreed we would view every gravesite until we met in the middle of the graveyard. We expected to find nothing, certainly not a pile of money. The grave markers told us that many people of bygone days were at rest there.

We had completed about two rows of cemetery plots each when I looked down to find a large pile of money glistening in the sun. I yelled for Sid. He came quickly and was rendered speechless at the sight. When we regained our senses, we took in the surroundings. Children played basketball less than a block away. Houses were in the vicinity. People walked on nearby streets. There was no way in the world that others didn't know about the money. Not only was it piled up in front of us, but our feet crunched on coins in the dirt as we walked around the grave marker. I didn't tamper with the grave, but Sid donated four quarters. The man buried there was named Percy Washington. We agreed we would not question the people at the city offices. After dining at our favorite restaurant in Beaufort, we drove back to Myrtle Beach.

Sometime later, I mentioned the money on the grave to a group at Bonnie Doone Plantation, near Walterboro and Beaufort, where I was a member of an Elderhostel faculty. Those attending the elderhostel program were from cities across the United States and several foreign countries. A man from New Orleans insisted that he see first-hand what I had talked about. Several of us rode with him in a van headed to Citizens Cemetery. Although he was familiar with strange beliefs and activities in his state, he had never seen anything like the spectacle. He took from the gravesite three greenish-oxidized dimes, one for each of his grandchildren, and replaced them with clean dimes. I warned him about violating the grave, but he insisted that his grandchildren would have something to show and tell for years.

In 1996, we again visited the Citizens Cemetery. The money was gone, and Mrs. Percy Washington had been laid to rest beside her husband. According to her grave marker, she had lived a hundred years, born in 1896 and buried in 1996. There was no question that it would be necessary to clear Percy Washington's grave of the money before Mrs. Washington could be laid to rest. Although no money lay on the graves, our feet still crunched on coins in the dirt.

As far as I know, there were no stockholders in the Percy Washington enterprise, and no stock certificates. Total assets had grown since the business of putting money on Washington's grave started but if dividends were declared, the general public knew nothing of it.

Nancy Rhyne

Questions and Answers with Aunt Liza

QUESTION: *Aunt Liza, when they moved the old Oatland Plantation church, the pillars were full of bees and honey, right?*
ANSWER: *Bees always were in that church.*
QUESTION: *Who built the church?*
ANSWER: *Old man Welcome Bease. Old man Welcome had a good memoranda.*
QUESTION: *Where were you married?*
ANSWER: *In the class room. White veil over my face. Wreath 'round my head.*
QUESTION: *Aunt Liza, your high cheekbones, gingerbread complexion and taciturn manner lead me to ask you if you have some Indian blood?*
ANSWER: *What kind of sick that been?*

Liza Small
Parkersville, South Carolina.
As told to Genevieve W. Chandler, WPA field worker 1937.

∾ ∽

Evacuation

I was born and raised on Wadmalaw Island and was the only one on this island when the Civil War began. Then, Maussa carried seventy of us slaves to Greenville, on account of its mountains, which Maussa believed would have prevented the Yankees from invading. The Yankees had gunboats but they were good only for water battles. Greenville didn't know what was going on.

Maussa didn't tell us anything. For about four years we stayed in Greenville. One morning the generals and colonels came a-riding into Greenville and ordered everybody to surrender. Not a gun was fired. We stayed there until harvest time. Then it was back to Wadmalaw Island and the usual punishment and the broad effects it had on us.

On Wadmalaw Island Maussa had three kinds of punishment for them that disobeyed him. One was the Sweet Box. They made it the height of the person and no larger. Just large enough so that the person could be squeezed in. The box was nailed and if it was summer it was put in the blazing sun. In winter it was put in the coldest, dampest and deepest place. The next punishment was the Stock. Wooden posts were nailed to the barn floor. The person being punished was stretched out on his back and the hands and feet were tied to the posts. The third

55

punishment was the Bilbo, where you were put on a high place and not stationed securely. If you fell you hurt yourself real bad if your neck wasn't broken.

Prince Smith
As told to Augustus Ladson, WPA field worker.
Charleston, South Carolina.

ᢙ ᢙ

Living With the Ghost of Aunt Sissy

Nancy Elizabeth Hickman, known by the family as Aunt Sissy, was born in 1868 at the family plantation at Hickman Branch, known today as Hickman's Crossroads, in North Myrtle Beach. She was named for her mother and her mother's maiden sister, Elizabeth Marlow. Her father, Lieutenant Thomas Hickman, served in the Civil War at the battle of Fort Fisher, near Wilmington, North Carolina. He was captured in January 1865 and spent four months in Elmira Prison in New York. After he was paroled, he walked home, and his health was never the same. He literally worked himself to death trying to support the family. He died in 1887. Her mother, Nancy Lenora Marlow, came from an old and distinguished family from Old Dock, in Columbus County, North Carolina.

When Nancy married in 1864, her husband brought her to live at Hickman Branch. Part of her dowry included five house servants who made the journey with her. The descendants of those Marlow servants still reside in the Hickman's Crossroads.

In 1878, Aunt Sissy came down with the fever. No one knows exactly which fever it was but family recollections say it was scarlet fever. Rhett, Aunt Sissy's sister, described how Aunt Sissy suffered due to the high fever. In between the chills and shakes, Aunt Sissy called for her mother. When her mother came, Sissy did not recognize her. After Aunt Sissy's death in 1878 she was buried in the family cemetery at Hickman Branch. Due to the family's reduced circumstances after the Civil War, a wooden marker served as Aunt Sissy's headstone. As the years passed, time and the elements eroded the marker away, leaving nothing behind. There is one item left as a reminder of Aunt Sissy, her portrait.

The portrait was completed between 1875 and 1878. A traveling artist/photographer happened by before Aunt Sissy was buried and captured her likeness as a memorial for the family. The picture shows a little girl attired in a white dress. She has dark brown curls secured by a white ribbon. Around her neck is an emerald pendant on a white ribbon. A gold and walnut frame with floral carvings encloses the picture. The portrait hung in the Hickman home until 1918 when Aunt Sissy's mother, Nancy Marlow Hickman, died. Rhett inherited the picture and later passed it on to her daughter Beulah Long Bennett.

David Bennett of Myrtle Beach, was introduced to Aunt Sissy in December 1985 when Beulah, his grandmother, was spending Christmas with her family in Wilmington, North Carolina. During Christmas dinner, family stories came up, including one about Aunt Sissy. When David saw Aunt Sissy's portrait, he was mesmerized. Later that afternoon his grandmother asked if he would like to have the portrait. Of course he wanted it. He had heard many strange stories about Aunt Sissy. David Bennett tells his story:

In 1997, when I moved into a new apartment I decided to hang Aunt Sissy in my living room. After realizing I had limited wall space, I decided to put her in a closet. Before doing so, I jokingly looked at the picture and said, "Sissy, I haven't any room for you on my walls. I've got to pack you away." Later that night I was awakened by someone or something hitting me on my left arm. I quickly rolled over just in time to see a girl in white leave the room. I eventually fell asleep and awoke several hours later, got up and checked to see if all the doors and windows were locked. There was no sign of forced entry. I figured it must have been a dream and got dressed. When I removed my shirt, I noticed a bruise on my left arm. The bruise was in the exact spot where I had been hit. I thought for a moment and then realized that Aunt Sissy did this. When I told her that I was putting her in the closet she must have gotten mad. Considering self-preservation I decided to hang Aunt Sissy in my living room. From then on I was never touched again. But the incidents didn't stop. One morning while making my lunch for the day, I heard a click, like a doorknob turning. The door to my bedroom slowly opened. I yelled, "All right, Sissy, stop it." The door stopped opening. Then it opened and closed. The only way I could get the door to act normal was to stop it halfway. After this incident, apparitions could be seen out of the corner of an eye, flashes of light leaving a room or the image of a small girl standing off to a side. However, when I turned to get a better view, there was nothing there. A friend from out of town spent a few nights at my house.

One morning after I left for work, he got up and turned on the TV. He went back to bed and fell asleep. When he awoke the TV was off, but my electric razor was on, in the bathroom. Zzzzz. In December 2001, I moved from my apartment to a townhouse I had purchased. After moving in, I hung Aunt Sissy along with other family portraits by the stairway. Once, after getting out of the shower, I looked towards the door and saw a little girl, dressed in white, staring at me. I closed my eyes and shook my head, and the image was gone. Another time a little girl came down the stairs and peered around the corner. Her reflection was clear in the plate glass of my open front door. A few days later I was washing dishes and heard what sounded like someone running down my stairs. The front door opened and closed. After a few moments, it opened again and someone ran up the stairs. Curiosity got the best of me so I rushed back to the front door. No one was in sight. I looked at the portrait and yelled, "All right, Sissy. You can't go out without my permission."

The spirit that lives within the portrait of Aunt Sissy isn't a mean one. It's a ten-year-old girl who likes to make her presence known. If she ever is forgotten or ignored, she will do something to remind me that she is still around. Every day I speak to Aunt Sissy and ask her how she is doing. Some of my friends think I'm crazy to speak to her, but those same people won't go near the portrait. Others believe perfectly. They always say "Hello Sissy" when they walk into my home. They know I live at home with Aunt Sissy.

Aunt Sissy still lives, but not at Hickman Branch.

David Bennett
As told to Nancy Rhyne in a personal interview.
Myrtle Beach, South Carolina.

ᐁ ᐁ

The Sea Monkey

In the 1930s Sabe Rutledge, a man who had been born in slavery, ran The Ark Fishery, at Floral Beach [today Surfside Beach]. The official name and address was posted on a sign in front of the fishing shack: *Burgess Post Office, Horry County, South Carolina.*

Sabe Rutledge sat high in his watchtower and scanned the ocean for schools of mullet. A large number of fish rode in on the waves now and then, giving the breakers a gray tint. That was when Uncle Sabe and his men ran down the steps of the lookout to their boats. The rowboats were heavy with nets. Each netting of mullet meant money in Uncle Sabe's pocket and food on his table. He said he ate nothing but mullet and rice for three months each fall.

Sabe was a storyteller. The first telling of the tales mostly always took place around a fire over which the fishermen fried several mullet in a large, black, cast-iron skillet. Sabe viewed many spectacles, including loggerhead turtles in June, meteors streaking across the sky on August nights, and various sea creatures that couldn't be accounted for. The old man sometimes took friends with him in his boat. He many times said, "I'm knocking off and going fishing today. You want to go?"

"Now you take that ocean there," Sabe said one day when he took his helpers and a boy fishing. "It makes you think. It makes *me* think! When I'm a-sitting up there in my lookout, I study the ocean. It's some great place to contain all that water. That ocean water goes somewhere at low tide, and it don't station itself anywhere. It just revolves and comes back, exploring. And I study that sea in my boat the same as I do when I'm in the lookout. I keep my eye open." The breakers jarred the boat, but Sabe kept on rowing. It was a rough ride until they cleared the breakers and were in open sea.

Sabe picked up a fishing pole, pealed away the fishing line and slipped the hook through a chunk of shrimp. The boat tilted as he moved around and vigorously threw the line into the water in back of the boat. He continued to row the boat. It moved forward. The bated fish hook slid through the water at the back.

"I hope you get a whopper," said a helper, not taking his eyes off the line.

"You never know what's in this sea," warned Sabe. "We can hook anything. But a mess o'mullet would be good for the supper table."

A boat coming in passed by. "Mornin', Sabe," a man called. "How you?"

"Oh, I ain't worth none a-tall," answered Sabe. "The rheumatism was right smart bothersome last night." He jerked his head as a symbol of futility and rowed even harder. In no time at all they were in deeper water.

Just then something jerked the fishing line.

"It's a big one," a man screamed. "Grab the pole, Sabe."

Sabe reached for the fishing pole. The whopper on the line pulled the cane pole into the shape of a half moon.

"Pull him in, Sabe," urged his friend. "Bring him on home."

"It's big. Is it a shark?" asked another.

"I don't know what it is, but it has hands, and no fish I've ever caught had hands," Sabe growled.

Two tiny hands with black fingers and fingernails pulled on the line.

"Get the net," called Sabe. "The net is under the bait box."

"It's a brown, fuzzy animal that has hands," the boy screamed.

Sabe threw the pole down and helped pull in the net, lugging with all his might.

"What is it?" the boy cried. "Is it a sea monster?"

"It's that and more," said Sabe through clinched teeth. It was clear that getting the monster out of the water was heavy-duty work.

Suddenly, the animal unexpectedly jumped into the boat. The fishing line hung from the animal's mouth, the hook still in his throat. The fishermen in the boat backed away, but they couldn't go far.

"What is it?"

"It's a critter all right. Believe it or not, it's a sea monkey."

"A sea monkey? I never heard of such a thing," a seasoned fisherman exclaimed.

"And I've never seen one. Get back. Don't let him bite you," Sabe cautioned.

The monkey was bad-tempered. It chattered a garbled noise as its black eyes darted from Sabe to the others.

"Monkeys are clever," warned Sabe. "His object is to get back into the sea, and we won't get in his way. I'll cut the line, and when he goes overboard, he'll be gone."

Sabe took a knife from his tackle box and cut the fishing line. As he predicted, the monkey jumped to the rim of the boat and then overboard and out of sight.

"Was it *really* a monkey?" asked the boy.

"You can't argue it from a monkey," said Sabe. "You saw that curled up tail and the way he moved his head, quick-like."

"And his feet," someone added.

"They were little nubs," said Sabe. "He worked those little nubs back and forth." Sabe reflected for a moment, then added, "Everything on earth is out there in that sea, and more. That's because there is more water than there is land."

He settled down, turned the boat around and headed toward home.

Sabe Rutledge had a new story to tell.

As told to Genevieve W. Chandler, WPA field worker.
Murrells Inlet, South Carolina 1937.

Once Upon A Time When Charleston Was The Capital

From 1670 to 1786 Charleston was the capital of South Carolina, and English nobles and Carolina aristocrats were governors during that period and beyond.

Until about 1760 the colonies were considered dependencies of the English Crown. Parliamentary supremacy was already established in England, and the system created in Charleston followed the English philosophy and tactics as the rule. Although English law was the basis of colonial government, administration of the colonies was the concern of the Crown. The royal prerogative and influence operated as a major force in developing American constitutions.

Of the several instruments of royal government, the most formal and authoritative was the charter. Usually a charter was perpetual during the granting king's reign, but it could be ended by voluntary surrender or through a judicial process. By one of these charters the region we call North and South Carolina was granted by Charles II of England to eight of his favorite lord proprietors. They were given extensive rights and privileges for the government of the province they immediately settled, but they were to legislate for the province by and with the advice, assent and approval of the Crown. The terms of the gift were payment to the king of one-fourth of the gold and silver found in the colony, a yearly rental of twenty marks, and his recognition as sovereign lord.

By the fundamental constitutions, the oldest proprietor in Carolina was to act as governor and at his decease was to be succeeded by the eldest of the survivors. If there was no resident proprietor, a governor was to be appointed by the palatine, or a majority of the proprietors on approval of the Crown. The palantine was to sit as president of the palatine's court and had the power to nominate and appoint the governor, who after obtaining the royal approval became his representative in Carolina.

For fifty years Charleston's history was that of the colony of South Carolina, of which it was the capital. The governor, his council and the assembly made up the governing body within the province. The governor's salary was always a matter of contention. Under proprietary rule he was paid two hundred pounds sterling a year, and then four hundred. In the royal era, he received a small salary from the king, augmented by an annual gift from the assembly, amounting in all to about five hundred pounds sterling. The transition to the royal government in 1719 gave South Carolina its freedom to unlock North and South Carolina.

In both the proprietary and royal periods, the office of governor was held only at the pleasure of the grantee (palatine or king) and on sufferance of the people, so the terms varied in length, ranging from a few months to several years. Columbia was founded as the capital in 1786, and began its actual career as the seat of state government with the convening of the legislature in the first unfinished statehouse on January 4, 1790.

The first of the Charleston governors was William Sayle. Although he was well suited for the job of governor, he was an old man, and his assistant Joseph West did most of the work. West became governor in 1671.

Compiled from the reports of WPA field workers
in Charleston, South Carolina.

∾ ∾

The Governor Who Rebuilt Charles Town

James Glen, who came as governor to the province in 1743, faced one of the most difficult jobs addressed by a royal governor. Arriving in the province shortly after a most disastrous fire had swept across Charles Town destroying every house that stood below the northern side of Broad Street, Governor Glen wrote to his secretary that having "found Charles Town in ashes," his dearest wish was to leave it fair, flourishing and fortified.

Although even the carriage guns in the fortifications and some of the bastions themselves were destroyed by the fire, so fine was the spirit of the people that they commenced the difficult task of rebuilding almost immediately, and by the time the governor arrived in 1743 the era of prosperity which was to endure for a long while had already set in.

That the wish for the welfare of the people entrusted to his care lay close to the heart of Governor Glen is shown in the selection of his exact words for the inscription on his coffin plate: He found them in ashes and left them fair, fortified and flourishing. This plate, attached to a marble tablet may be seen in the Statehouse in Columbia today.

Compiled from the reports of WPA field workers
in Charleston, South Carolina.

The Mace

William Henry Lyttleton, governor of South Carolina 1756–1760, brought the lovely mace that is still in use today. Many interesting stories are told of the extraordinary silver and burnished in gold mace. This symbol of authority has lain upon the Speaker's Table in the South Carolina House of Representatives for about two hundred and fifty years. It is believed by some to be none other than Oliver Cromwell's famous "bauble."

On the panels of this beautiful piece of silver are the royal arms of Great Britain, the arms of the House of Hanover and the arms of the province of South Carolina. The remaining panels show other interesting insignia.

This mace is believed to be the only one in the United States, which antedates the revolution. It was crafted by Magdalen Feline, who was renowned for the beauty and excellence of her work in making silver ceremonial staffs.

Compiled from the reports of WPA field workers
in Charleston, South Carolina.

∾ ∽

Governor Sails with Another Man's Wife

It may be difficult to imagine anything untoward would be connected with the governors and other Charlestonians in these gilded days of powdered wigs, brocaded waistcoats, knee britches and silver buckles on their shoes. On May 14, 1764, a caption that raised eyebrows might very properly have appeared in South Carolina papers. On that day Thomas Boone, the quarrelsome governor, abandoned his people and embarked for England. He did not sail alone. His traveling companion was a lady of high-social standing in the community—a woman who was another man's wife. She was Mrs. Samuel Peronneau, the former Sarah Ann Tattnall, a granddaughter of the first John Barnwell of South Carolina.

In due process of time, Mr. Peronneau obligingly died and Thomas and Sarah Ann remedied their anomalous state by a regular marriage ceremony.

Compiled from the reports of WPA field workers
in Charleston, South Carolina.

∾ ∽

All Modern Conveniences

Twenty-five-year old royal governor Lord Charles Greville Montagu (1766–1768) became so disgusted with the old-fashioned inconveniences of his house that he packed up and moved over to Fort Johnson on James Island. There he spoke of erecting a castle befitting the dignity of his office. This proper governor's mansion, however, never was built. The governors who followed Governor Montagu had to content themselves with the conveniences of the modern American home of that day. Although Governor Montagu never built his castle in the clouds, he did lay the cornerstone of South Carolina's first lighthouse.

The United States accepted the Charleston Lighthouse from the State of South Carolina with the act of August 7, 1789. It took over the joint jurisdiction of all the seacoast lighthouses of the infant nation. Several lighthouses have stood in that same dark angle of the waters. When the second lighthouse was being dismantled to make room for the third a lead plate was found on which was a tracing of the first little lighthouse. In the cornerstone was also a copper plate inscribed with the names of the king of England George III; the governor of the province Lord Charles Greville Montagu; the Lieutenant Governor William Bull; the commissioners; the architect; the engineer; the clerk and the bricklayer of the building.

Compiled from the reports of WPA field workers
in Charleston, South Carolina.

A Most Romantic Royal Governor

The younger son of the Duke of Argyle and the last of South Carolina's royal governors Lord William Campbell must have been of a most romantic nature, for scarcely had he arrived in the province in the spring of 1763, when he met Miss Sara Izard, daughter of a wealthy South Carolina planter, and fell head over heels in love with her. After a brief courtship, on the 7th of April 1763, he married the young lady, and the couple embarked upon the *Nightingale* for an unknown destination. The young husband was indeed a fortunate person, for besides being really in love with his wife, Miss Sara brought with her a dowry of 50,000 pounds sterling.

Compiled from the reports of WPA field workers
in Charleston, South Carolina.

Mr. Waterson's Legacy

In spite of the activities of pirates along the coast of South Carolina, there are few surviving legends about vast hoards of their buried gold. There may have been a few small and sporadic searches organized among the islanders, but there has been no bit of fact or legend sufficiently alluring to entice a real expedition.

The most fascinating of surviving legends of unfound treasure concerns the fortune of a Mr. Waterson, who lived in Charleston in the 1850s. Judging from the legend, he must have been a man with an ironical sense of humor. Having amassed a considerable fortune in property and money, he realized that he had no relatives closer than a few cousins whom he heartily despised.

On a certain memorable day, Mr. Waterson called a conclave of these voracious cousins who were hovering about waiting for his death. They all met at the home of Mr. Waterson, a little house near Church Street located on Tradd Street. There he gleefully informed them that they were waiting in vain if they hoped to spend any of his money. He assured them that not one of them would ever grasp a cent of his fortune, for he had placed it where neither the sun nor the moon would ever shine upon it.

After Mr. Waterson's demise, his heirs took a loan on his property and used the money to dismantle his house and look in every nook and cranny. No money was found. They had the grounds around the house dug and the soil examined, but not a penny was there. As Mr. Waterson had envisioned, the sun and moon has not shined on a cent of his fortune.

∾ ↬

Daughter of a Sea Captain

My name is Nancy Farrior Jussely Lyle. Daddy was Captain John Edward Jussely, who spent seventy-five interesting sea-faring years. It would take quite a volume to do justice to such a fascinating life. Daddy's operation of the Hildegarde *began first by hauling freight and passengers between Savannah and Charleston. After 1923, he was captain of a Charleston to Beaufort run with harbor cruises and excursions. Later he operated a passenger and freight service between Charleston and Sullivan's Island* [this was when there was no connecting bridge]. *Toward the end of Daddy's career, he spent a few summers as captain of a deep sea fishing vessel at Myrtle Beach. Daddy renewed his Master's License and loved those times at Myrtle Beach whenever a Master's License was necessary to take a fishing vessel beyond the allowed limit. After a few more summers spent as captain of a deep sea fishing vessel at Myrtle Beach, Daddy and Mama lived to the end of Mama's life at their wonderful home "Harbor View," at Mt. Pleasant, overlooking the Charleston Harbor. Daddy enjoyed every ship of which he was captain, but I believe the* Hildegarde *was his favorite.*

The Hildegarde*'s papers show she was built of wood in 1898 at Westerly, Rhode Island. She had a registered length of 90 feet, breadth of 19 feet, depth of 6.2 feet and a gross tonnage of 149.65. She was purchased in 1922 from the Savannah & Bluffton Steamboat Company for "coasting trade." Mama saw to the purchase while Daddy was on one of his long sea*

voyages. Daddy was immediately in command and had advertising cards printed with these words: For Charter – Day or Night – Excursions, Picnics or Moonlight Sails. Capacity 300. For rates phone 2767. Daddy said Mama bought the vessel for him to keep him closer to home. They couldn't hold each other close enough.

When Daddy married Mama, Miss Clara Virginia Hinson, she was the director of the public kindergarten in Savannah. They had three daughters. Daddy allowed us children to travel with him on some of his voyages. I didn't realize until recently that Isabel was always homesick on her trips without Mama, but I loved every minute. I was completely at home aboard ship and loved the sights, sounds and smells—the lapping of the water against the ship's sides at nighttime. I remember well the faithful greeting from Felix de Weldon's famous Savannah's Waving Girl sculpture as the Hildegarde passed in and out of the Savannah harbor.

The Inland Waterway from Savannah to Charleston was about 150 miles. It was a beautiful maze of sea islands. The banks were lined with mighty oaks and lofty pines, draped with Spanish moss. There were places where the Waterway would narrow so that you could almost grasp the rushes and reeds. Navigation of a vessel the size of the Hildegarde *was quite a feat and kept Daddy straining at the wheel.*

On a voyage to Beaufort during the time of an unusually high tide, the Hildegarde *ran aground, her keel broke, and a high tide took her down into the salt tides. She sank heart-wounded. Not even the piano was saved. Sea captains are intrepid sailors. The blood of passage continued to burn in Daddy's veins.*

During World War II, Daddy taught navigation at the Fort Sumter Hotel in Charleston. He also spent time during that war as captain on Coast Guard and Merchant Marine vessels. He once related to me that, in addition to cargo, he was to take aboard a few recent graduates of the U.S. Naval Academy to ships in North Africa. At mealtime one of the midshipmen came to Daddy to ask where the officers were to dine. There were no arrangements except with the crew. Daddy immediately told them they were fortunate to have a choice—since there was a war going on they could either dine with the crew or do without! They found seats with the crew and enjoyed their meals.

My precious Mama stayed at home while Daddy was at sea during World War II. We didn't know about the experiences Daddy was having until he returned and told us the stories. He said that one day a German sub surfaced, knocking his captain's stool from under him. The blimp following his ship scared the sub away. Daddy escaped unharmed, except minor injuries to his leg while tumbling down the steep steps to the pilot house. He was taken to a hospital in Bermuda to recuperate. His assessment of this incident was, "The Good Lord is not through with me yet."

Daddy remembered once when being transferred by train for command to another ship, he called Mama to have her meet him at the North Charleston Station. His crewmen were all watching from the train windows. Daddy strode off the train, in uniform, in full command and immediately, as he joined us, broke into tears and couldn't utter a word. He had to turn his back on his crew throughout the five-minute meeting.

Mama and Daddy left us with more memories than if they had lived a thousand years, but we went on to make our own memories. I married David Lyle. He was an attorney and served as mayor of Rock Hill for fourteen years. The Dave Lyle Boulevard in Rock Hill is named in his honor. Our three daughters gave us wonderful memories and grandchildren.

Nancy Farrior Jussely Lyle
As told to Nancy Rhyne.
Rock Hill, South Carolina.

ରେ ৩৯

The Secret of Brick House Plantation

It is said of Elizabeth Jenkins Young, who lives on Charleston's famous Meeting Street, that her love of Charleston guides her life. That may be true, but when I chatted with her on March 1, 2004, I would have been hard-pressed to find any subject of which she is more enamored than Brick House, her home on Edisto Island. Although we were talking on the phone, I believed it took only two minutes for tears to well in her eyes. Mrs. Young refers to herself as Aunt Lizzie, the matriarch of Brick House. Her narrative began in 1720, when Brick House was built by Paul Hamilton, the grandfather of South Carolina governor and President James Madison's appointed secretary of the navy Paul Hamilton III. According to Mrs. Young, the brick for the house was made in Holland, where a finer and sturdier quality was produced than plantation-made brick. Forty thousand bricks were used in the chimneys, and there is no other brick like it in South Carolina. All lumber used in construction of the house was cut on another of Hamilton's plantations. Before it was used in the building of the house it was seasoned seven years. The carpenters, people born in slavery, were gifted in their trade. Although the mansion lies in ruins today, at one time the high-pitched roof soared over rooms filled with valuable paintings that were the envy of the strongly rooted Charlestonians. In 1798, Brick House passed into the hands of the Jenkins family. The Jenkins men played important parts in the Revolutionary and Civil Wars.

I could feel Mrs. Young's sadness when she explained that Brick House burned on January 29, 1929.

I was born in Brick House and was seven years old when it burned. None of us ever got over it. The roof was slate installed over shingles. The fire started under the roof, in the attic. The slate was so

hot. So very hot. Slates were flying everywhere. We rushed out and didn't save a toothbrush. The fire was so tragic. The interior rooms were magnificent and the valuable paintings cannot be replaced.

Daddy was a widower with five children when he came to Edisto and met Mother. Mother moved to Edisto after the death of her fiancé. He died by electrocution. Mother and Daddy were married and had three children. I was one of the three. All eight of the children were very close. We loved each other. The children inherited houses at Edisto, and we all go there for the summer. Some of the houses are near the ruins of Brick House and some of them are not so close. Someone is in every one of the houses during the summer. My grandchildren and great-grands go. All families just love Edisto Island. The river is wonderful for fishing, crabbing, boating, and we all go out to eat at the best places. We all cherish Brick House and we cherish each other. We formed a Brick House Trust group, and we all adhere to that. We meet in June, and everybody comes to the island.

Mother stored away all documents including the grant from King Charles dated 1698. Mother knew I would take care of it. Brick House includes the marsh and most land grants did not include the marsh area. After the fire, people from across the country were interested in Brick House and obtained information about it. The Library of Congress made blueprints of everything about Brick House. They have documents of everything. The South Carolina Historical Society has Brick House papers.

Mrs. Young remembers an Edisto Island when there was no bridge to the mainland. "Someone came and said they wanted to build a bridge to Edisto Island. All of us who lived here said we wanted to keep everyone who lived on the island, and as to the people who did not live here, we didn't want them."

At the age of 16, Mrs. Young went to the College of Charleston. She said a four-year education at that college cost her father $500.00. "And we didn't have to buy our books because they were furnished."

Many people visit the ruins of Brick House on Edisto Island, but the house has a secret that few know about.

When a child of the Brick House Plantation family dies, and the remaining family members mourn at the ruins of Brick House, a substantial portion of the ruins falls away. Elizabeth Jenkins Young said it always happens. What is left of the house makes a contribution to the moment.

We gather at Trinity Episcopal Church for the funeral and the burial in the cemetery. After that, we go back to Brick House to feel the harmony and sweet sensations of the house and each other. More than once, during this time of powerful feelings and solitude, a part of the ruins tumbles into our midst.

We buried my brother at Trinity Episcopal Church and we all went back to Brick House, as we always do after a funeral. While we stood there, a part of a window fell to the ground. We were not surprised. It happens every time.

It is a twist that feels appropriate that when a child of Brick House dies the house makes a sacrifice. The Jenkins family's love of each other and what is left of the house reveals truths about some Edisto icons, but the secret of Brick House remains locked within.

Elizabeth Jenkins Young
As told to Nancy Rhyne in a personal interview.
Charleston, South Carolina.

Poinsettia Named for Lowcountryman

Casa Bianca, the home of the famous Joel Poinsett, stood on the point of land between the Pee Dee and Black Rivers, in Georgetown County. This plantation was acquired by Poinsett through marriage with the widow of John Julius Pringle, formerly one of the wealthy Izard girls, who spent her summers in Newport and her winters in Washington. She was a woman of charm and originality, and is said to have introduced in New York the fashion of wearing small, live snakes as bracelets at the opera. That the Izard women were always remarkable is shown by the celebrated witticism passed in Washington on one of them by a lady who declared, in speaking of the Bee and Izard families that they were "a proud lot from B to Z."

In connection with these aristocratic people, it is of interest that Mary Pringle, daughter of Mr. and Mrs. Julius Izard Pringle, whose mother was a Miss Lynch, and whose home was Greenfield, on the Black River, several miles northwest of Chicora Wood Plantation, married into nobility, her husband being Count Ivan des Frances. Another family place was Weymouth, on the Pee Dee River, six miles south of Chicora Wood, the residence of Mr. and Mrs. Ralph Izard, the latter having been a Miss Pinckney.

Joel Poinsett was a Charlestonian of national or even international reputation. His home had always been in the city of Charleston until his retirement from public life. A local notice in a Charleston paper in 1832 mentions his father in an account of the celebration of St. George's Day by the "Fort Jolly Volunteers" at the "House of Trooper Poinsett, their usual house of rendezvous." The son's residence was situated on what is now Rutledge Avenue, a few squares above Calhoun Street on the west side. The house was a plain wooden one with columns in front, having somewhat the exterior appearance of a small church. It was recessed some distance from the street, and stood in the midst of a grove of live oaks. It was generally known as "Poinsett's Grove," and had probably been a farm before the city limits extended so far.

Poinsett had traveled much, and had observed in the cities of Europe the great usefulness of galleries of paintings and statues, their improvement and elevation of the tastes of the people, and with the hope of starting such an institution in Charleston he obtained land on Broad Street west of Logan from the Methodist church as the site of his proposed "Academy of Fine Arts." This was done in 1833, and he also got pictures and statues. If Poinsett's plan was not permanently successful it was at least a great step forward, and is realized in the Gibbes Museum of Art on Meeting Street.

Poinsett was awarded for his great interest in science by having a beautiful flower named for him. It was described by two botanists, Wildenow and Graham, without its being known exactly which one had priority. The first called Euphorbia Pulcherrima, and the second Poinsettea Pulcherrima. It belongs to the family of Euphorbiacia, is a native of Mexico, and was discovered there about the year 1828. It is commonly known, however, as the poinsettia.

Annie Ruth Davis, WPA field worker.
Marion, South Carolina.

Murder at the Ten Mile House

Brother Creightsburg was an itinerant Methodist preacher traveling on horseback to Charleston in the latter part of the eighteenth century. Caught at dusk ten miles from his destination, he decided to tarry for the night at a tavern he was approaching. Over the door swung a lantern that illuminated a sign that read "Ten Mile House." He dismounted and handed his reins to the stable boy. He was thinking about the bowl of Hoppin' John he would order once he was seated in the dining room.

Brother Creightsburg gave his order and while waiting for the food to arrive he began to feel the fatigue of having traveled a long distance. He ate his meal and retired early, immediately falling asleep. How much time had elapsed he did not know but he awakened startled. Hearing gasps and a noise of struggling in the next room, he climbed on a chair and peered over the transom. What he saw filled him with horror.

Two legs protruded from one side of a folding bed. His eyes registered convulsive kicking of those legs. From the other side of the bed an arm, the hand opening and shutting, fingers twitching spasmodically, distracted his eyes from the legs. The air was full of noises—gasps and wheezing sounds.

The host rested himself on top of the folded mattress. His wife sat there too. While the preacher gazed like one hypnotized, the struggles ceased. The two arose. Opening the folded bed the host disclosed the bluish, contorted features of their victims. While the hostess went through the victim's pockets in search of what filthy lucre there might be, Brother Creightsburg, regaining the use of his limbs, tip-toed to the window. Out he went. The stable was found. In his little nightie he mounted his steed. In the gray of early morning he rode into Charleston. Apparently the shock had temporarily upset his mental equilibrium. For some days his sole remark or answer to questions was rather indefinite, unsatisfying. Later, when he was normal, he told his tale. Upon investigation several bodies were found in the cellar in quick-lime. That the host and hostess paid the penalty on the gallows for their crimes is illustrative of how sure and swift was punishment meted out in that day and time.

Genevieve W. Chandler, WPA field worker.
Murrells Inlet, South Carolina.

ↄ ↄ

The Great Sea Turtle

The loggerhead turtles that live on the South Carolina coast belong to the reptile family, and they are one of the few reptiles still living which wandered the earth's water before man was created. Its body, two feet in length, is covered with plates of shell, dark brown on the back and pale yellow underneath. It has a very large head and long neck, which can be drawn into the shell or stretched out a foot or more. The four powerful flippers are used for swimming and digging in the sand and can be folded back against the shell. Its tail is very small, about six or eight inches long. Few people know about the burrs and thorns in the life of the loggerhead turtle.

Early in March while the salt air is still nipping cold, these turtles leave the ocean for the little creeks and inlets along the coast. It is here in the quiet waters that they breed. Day after day they are seen in pairs floating near the surface of the creeks. Food also is plentiful, for at this time of the year crabs are preparing to spawn along the mud banks of the creeks. The powerful horned jaws of the turtle make short work of a crab, easily crunching the shell so that it can be swallowed.

As the warmer days of May come the turtles leave the sheltered creeks behind the coastal islands for the open ocean. It is from the ocean that they crawl out onto the beaches to lay their eggs.

All day and all night the waves roll on the sandy beaches along the coast. The tides are high and low. The moon shines or is shut away by clouds. The wind and rain lash the beach. The turtle doesn't notice. Through the summer, at periods of ten or twelve days, she crawls out on the beach to lay her eggs.

Dusk had just fallen when such a turtle slowly pushed her way out of the water. She had used the fore flippers only while swimming, but on the sand her rear flippers are brought into service. She begins to scan the sand dunes some two hundred feet away, leaving a track, which looked like the wake of a fast moving boat on its way to sea. Here the sand hills prove too high for her to climb and she drags her huge two hundred and fifty pound body back to the water to try at some other point for just the right place to dig a nest. This time the sand hills are high enough but not too high to climb, and in a place just above the high water mark she settles down to work.

She pushes her body from side to side making a hole the size of her shell and about a foot deep. Very carefully the right rear flipper is passed to her left side where she scoops some sand away from underneath her tail. The left flipper takes its turn making the same moves. The flippers finish their job and the hole is about ten inches deep and ten inches across. The turtle doesn't bother to look at the hole.

She sits on the hole for twenty minutes. Eggs drop every five or ten seconds, sometimes as many as three at a time. The turtle's head lies stretched far out of her shell and flat on the sand. Nothing disturbs her now.

The mature eggs are soon laid and she is ready to cover the nest, a secret place that she doesn't want others to know. She gathers some sand and packs it around the eggs. Then she does her muddling. As she crawls inland from the nest, she throws the sand against the wind; the wind throws it back again, haphazardly. It's a great structured force that makes for muddlement, one of the very sharpest elements of the procedure.

She rests for a second, but time tugs at the exhausted chain and pulls it back to start again the wondrous plan. Her exhaustion doesn't slow her down as she travels back to the water. Before fifteen days pass she will return to the beach and go through the process again, giving it her all. Within two months her babies bump themselves out of the shell and fight their way through the sand that has protected them. They are in the open now and danger lurks: raccoons, crabs, beachcombers. Those that make it to the water will not be on the beach again until they dig their nests, lay their eggs, and go back home.

Gardiner H. Walker, WPA field worker.
Charleston, South Carolina

~ ~

The Gift

Mr. Garland Outlaw, Horry County Game Warden, had a mule plowing in the field. He noted that there was a ragged, jagged fat lightard stump in the way of the animal and in some fashion he stumbled and fell and jabbed that stump in his side. The blood began to spurt like water from a flowing well. The veterinary came. He felt around in there trying to get a hold on a vein so as to stop that flow. And 'bout that time the mule must have lost three gallons of blood. Somebody up and said, "If it's your intention to save this mule you'd better send for Joe Brown quick."

"How's that?" the veterinary asked.

And the man up and told how Joe Brown could say a verse out of the Bible and stop a flow of blood right now. So Garland said if he was to be got he would get him.

In no time at all here he came and Joe just squatted down in front of the critter and looked him square in the eyes and said that verse three times and before Joe stopped reciting that verse the blood just turned off short like somebody had cut off a spigot. He said it like a prayer. Sounded like he was a-praying.

Others in the community learned the verse and they, too, were called on to stop a flow of blood. One of them explained how the gift worked. I found myself repeating that Bible verse over and over. Now I didn't have too much confidence in that verse, but one day we were fifteen miles up the coast and more miles than that from a doctor. We were cutting down a tree, and the saw went right through the pulse of a man's arm. Blood shot out just you stuck a hog. While I repeated the verse over and over, some other men shaved bark off a tree and pasted the shaved-up bark over the cut. That verse sure stopped the flow of blood. Now I can tell you what the verse is, but it'll only stop blood if certain ones say it. I've got that verse marked. It's the sixteenth chapter of Ezekiel, the sixth verse.

And when I passed by thee, and saw thee polluted in thine own blood, I said unto thee when thou wast in thy blood, Live; yea, I said unto thee when thou wast in thy blood, Live. *Ezekiel 16:6, King James Version.*

As told to Genevieve W. Chandler, WPA field worker.
Murrells Inlet, South Carolina 1937.

Before and After Freedom

My name is Gib McCormick, and I am a trustee of Socastee Graded School. I was staying in the house with a woman and she told me about that verse and I learned it. Not so long after I was following a bunch of timber hands sawing trees in the woods. I was a saw filer. They had cut down a big tree and had to turn the saw upside down and saw from the bottom and some way when they had got it sawed clean through it flirted up when they had to change the saw and one tooth of the saw cut through the pulse of a timberman's arm. Blood streamed off.

Of course I found myself repeating over and over that Bible verse and at the same time another man went to work shaving down bark and pasting some of it over the cut.

Now I didn't have too much confidence in that verse but the blood flow stopped and the man's life was saved. We were far away in the deep woods and no doctor was in that vicinity.

As told to Genevieve W. Chandler, WPA field worker.
Murrells Inlet, South Carolina 1937.

∾ ∿

Tokened

I've heard my mother tell about that. Her grandmother was tokened. Her grandmother's brother worked turpentine. Rode the woods. He hadn't been home in eighteen months and Ma's grandmother got a letter as how he was coming home. He hadn't been home in over a year. And she read the letter and told everybody as how he said he was coming home.

The day finally came that he was due home. Mama's grandma she was sitting out in the shade under a tree in the yard and she saw somebody walking around the house corner and she looked up and it was her brother. He went on around behind the house. She called his name and said, "Come here! I'm around here." And when he didn't come she went on around the house and there wasn't nobody there. When here Pa come to the house she told him they were going to get bad news. Sure enough the next day a letter came saying her brother was killed and thrown into the river.

This was way back there in turpentine days and he rode horseback all over a big scope of woods. Somebody killed him and threw him in the river.

Mama always said her grandmother was tokened.

As told to Genevieve W. Chandler, WPA field worker.
Murrells Inlet, South Carolina 1937.

ה‎

$\mathcal{C\!\!\!\!\sim}\ \mathcal{\!\!\!\sim\!\!\!o}$

The Disappearance of Theodosia Burr

On a bright December morning in 1812, the white sails of the *Patriot* glistened in the sunlight as she moved over the choppy waters of Georgetown harbor. A reconditioned privateer, her guns hidden below deck, the fast stepping little vessel was making a dash for New York, there to dispose of the rich spoils taken during raids on British ships.

Among the passengers on deck were a beautiful, dark-eyed lady, and a fashionably dressed gentleman, with great sidewhiskers. A little black and tan dog frisked about their feet, eagerly sniffing the strange sea smells.

Once again South Carolina's first lady, Theodosia Burr Alston, was going to New York to visit her father, Aaron Burr. Governor Joseph Alston was unable to leave the state at that time and accompany his wife on the voyage. For the second time the United States was at war with England. As commander of the forces in South Carolina, duty held him there. Moreover, the law at that time forbade the governor to leave the boundaries of the state during his term of office. It was a perilous voyage upon which Theodosia was embarking but he strongly felt that a visit with her father would improve her health, which had declined since the death of their only child six months earlier. Weak and frail from sorrow, Theodosia looked forward to the visit with her father, whom she had not seen since that day four years ago when he had fled to Europe. Although he had been cleared of the charge of treason, Burr still had so many bitter enemies that it had seemed best for him to go abroad. Now that he had returned, he wanted his beloved daughter. At noon the bar was reached. Governor Alston bade his wife farewell, cautioned her body servant to keep a close eye on her, and stepped into the boat waiting to bear him back to shore.

As he watched the *Patriot* grow smaller and smaller until he could no longer view her, Alston was worried. Winter is a dangerous time to sail the waters of the Atlantic. He knew that it was a perilous voyage upon which Theodosia had ensued. The British fleet was blockading the coast. He had heard some dock workers talk of a storm at sea. Worse still, pirates were lurking in the waters, ready to pounce on any unlucky ship that came their way. Certainly a land voyage would have been safer. But the trip by land took twenty days. The roads were rough, often impassable. Only stout hearts and healthy bodies could stand the rocking and jolting of the uncomfortable carriages and coaches of that day. The governor had given Captain Overstocks a letter to the commander of the blockading fleet, requesting a safe passage for the *Patriot*. It was all that he could do. He could not control the pirates. Finally he left the haunted air of the sea and went home.

Joseph Alston was a wealthy man. His grandfather, wealthy rice planter William Alston, had left him a substantial inheritance and he and Theo owned more than one plantation. The people born in slavery were fond of South Carolina's First Lady and after the death of her son they had waited on her hand and foot. They helped her with her medication and even suggested some of the herbs and roots they believed would help in restoring her to her health. She returned their acts of grace and acquired a reputation for kindness to the women who waited on her. These very women were in anguish over Theodosia's whereabouts and the safety of the vessel.

On New Year's Day a terrific storm struck the coast of North Carolina.

In New York an aged man paced the Battery, gazing eagerly out to sea. It was Aaron Burr, yearning for his daughter. Anxiously he scanned each sail that entered the harbor. Many ships came and went. But the *Patriot* never reached port.

Thirty days passed. The journey should only have taken five. In Georgetown Governor Alston gave up hope.

Tales began to be told of pirate capture, and imprisonment. Aaron Burr did not believe them and never gave up hope. He had to admit that if she were alive, all the prisons in the world would not keep her from her father. The weeks merged into months and then years.

Joseph Alston died, a broken hearted man, on September 10, 1816. Aaron Burr lived for many years, but life held no zest for him with Theo, his only child, gone. He said, "When I realized the truth of her death, the world became a blank to me."

Years after her disappearance General Thomas Pinckney, commander of all American forces south of Virginia, was in England. There he met the British admiral who had been in command of the blockading fleet. The talk turned to the *Patriot* and her beautiful passenger. The little ship had been stopped by the fleet, he said, but had been permitted to proceed when Governor Alston's letter was presented. The admiral said that the fleet itself had been scattered by the hurricane, which struck the coast that night. He felt sure that the pilot-boat could not have weathered the gale.

For years all sorts of tales were told of Theodosia's disappearance. Stories of her mysterious disappearance and deathbed confessions of pirates who said they caused her death when she was forced to walk the plank were the most popular. Several dying men claimed to have tilted the plank from which she walked into the sea. Proof was presented by all sorts of persons for all kinds of tales.

Dominique You, the favorite lieutenant of the notorious pirate, Jean Lafitte, who operated in the waters in and around New Orleans and the West Indies, said that at one time he was in Charleston. Dominique was a Creole of Santo Domingo. He was short and heavy as a stone, with fair hair, but his skin was so tanned it looked like leather.

Years passed. Dominique You became ill. He sent for a doctor, who told him he was a very sick man.

"How many days have I to live?" asked the pirate.

"Very few," was the reply.

The pirate began to tell the doctor the story of his life, a little every day. Finally he came to the story of Theodosia Burr. He spoke of meeting a small schooner near Cape Hatteras, off the North Carolina coast, on the 3rd of January, 1813. The ship, he said, was named the *Patriot*. She had recently been dismantled in a storm. As her guns had all been stored below, she was an easy prey for the pirate crew. Swiftly they boarded her. Brutally they murdered every man on board. Then the pirates dashed down to the cabins. They reappeared soon, dragging with them a woman of "surpassing beauty, deadly pale."

When questioned she said that she was Theodosia Burr, daughter of Aaron Burr, and wife of Joseph Alston, governor of South Carolina.

"A grand conquest," cried the pirates. With a shout they gathered around her. You said that she retreated with a look of "queenly dignity," but with no outward sign of fear.

When told that she must walk the plank, Theodosia calmly said: "I am ready; the sooner done, the better for me and for yourself."

You then had the plank laid out. Theodosia stepped upon it with unhurried grace, and descended into the sea, "as if she were alighting from a carriage."

In Alexandria, Virginia, in St. Paul's burying ground is a grave supposed by residents to be that of Theodosia Burr. A willow tree shades a simple slab on which these words appear: "To the memory of a female stranger, whose mortal sufferings terminated on the 14th day of October 1816, aged 23 years and 8 months. This stone was placed here by her disconsolate husband."

The cemetery is the favorite promenade of Alexandrians on Sunday afternoons. They love to gather around the willow-shaded grave, where they tell and retell this story.

Many years later, when Alexandria was a thriving port, two strangers arrived in the city. One was a lady, dark complexioned, very beautiful and evidently an American. The man, thought to be her husband, was English in appearance. They registered at the City Hotel.

A few days later the lady became ill. A doctor was sent for.

On his arrival the gentleman laid a pair of pistols on the table. "Do not be inquisitive," he commanded the doctor. "Ask her no questions about her family.

Before and After Freedom

Treat her for her disease and cure her if you can, but if you ask her any questions not relating to her bodily trouble, I shall blow your head off."

The lady died and was buried. The willow was planted and the slab put in place. The unknown gentleman returned several times to visit the grave. He always held himself aloof from everyone, and told no one his identity. If he were actually Governor Alston he never revealed the fact.

Many ships have gone down on the long sand dunes that edge the North Carolina coast, from Currituck to Cape Lookout. Sometimes the sea in stormy weather cuts its way between these strips of yielding sand to form new inlets.

On the peninsulas thus formed, in the early days of the 19th century lived bands of men called wreckers or bankers. Cut off from the rest of the world by the swirling surf, which almost encircled them, the wreckers were governed by laws of their own making. Not only did they believe that they had a right to all that the sea cast up, but also the right to actually wreck vessels and murder the crew, in order to get hold of their treasure. These men were really land pirates.

Many years after the disappearance of the *Patriot*, two criminals were put to death at Norfolk, Virginia. Before their execution they confessed that they had belonged to a gang of bankers who wrecked and robbed the *Patriot*, and had forced everyone on board, including Theodosia Burr, to walk the plank.

A band of these bankers lived at Nags Head, North Carolina. This little settlement was so called because of the pirates' habit of hanging lanterns about the neck of an old nag, which they drove up and down the beach on stormy nights. Ships at sea were fooled by the bobbing lights, which they took to be other vessels riding safely at anchor. Sailing on wit confidence, they ran aground on the dangerous banks of Nags Head and Kitty Hawk, two miles below. Then the land pirates murdered the members of the crew and robbed the vessel.

How the *Patriot* was lured on shore by the old nag, and Theodosia made to walk the plank, has been vividly told in a poem, illustrated with life-like pictures.

By the end of the 19th century Nags Head had become respectable. Pirates had been succeeded by summer visitors. Nags Head had become a surf-bathing resort. Among the usual vacation visitors was Dr. Poole, a highly respected physician of Elizabeth City, North Carolina.

One day the doctor was called on to prescribe for an ignorant old woman who lived in a little cabin near the coast. This old woman had been the widow of two bankers. On the wall of her humble dwelling hung an oil painting of a very beautiful woman, with piercing black eyes and olive skin. This portrait caught the eye of the doctor at once, on account of the resemblance it bore to a portrait of Theodosia Burr, which he had once seen and admired. The doctor was a student of national affairs and had long been interested in her fate.

He questioned the woman about the portrait. She explained how it came into her possession. One day, she said, when the United States was at war with England, a pilot-boat drifted near land, about two miles from Nags Head, with all sails set and rudder lashed.

The men (among them the man she later married) stopped their work and ran down to the shore. They boarded the ship. Not a soul was to be seen. The only living creature on board was a little black and tan dog. Everything was in order. The table was set for a meal. There were no signs of violence anywhere.

The bankers plundered the vessel and divided the spoil. Her sweetheart selected a lady's silk dress, which he found hanging in a closet in one of the cabins, an ornament of wax flowers, and this portrait, for his share, and gave these things to her.

Seeing the doctor's interest in the painting the old woman later gave it to him in gratitude for his services.

After the doctor came into possession of this portrait the excitement over Theodosia's disappearance started all over again. Many persons were convinced that it was a picture of her. They believed that Theo was taking it to her father. When Aaron Burr went to Europe he carried with him wherever he went a painting of his daughter. It had become faded and worn by much rolling during his travels. These people now said that the portrait was a new one, which Theodosia a taking him to replace the old.

The mysterious painting is on wood. It is 18 by 20 inches in size. The hair is auburn, the eyes piercing, and complexion olive, and it is said to be a striking resemblance to Theodosia Burr. A very lovely face of a woman in white, serene and sweet, it seems to wish to tell you something. But the secret of the painting has never been solved.

As recently as 1937 another "confession" appeared in a newspaper, but careful and dependable historians and writers feel that she was not captured by pirates, but went down in the January storm.

Millicent B. Hume, WPA field worker.
Charleston, South Carolina 1940.

Bullice Wine and Snakes

You talk black snake? They'll run you all right! Run the socks offen you. But then they are not so serious as the coach-whip snake. Coach-whip'll tie you down and whip you. My cousin Jake knew a man to Bucksport who had an uncle who got run by a coach-whip. He was an elder in the church, or a deacon, and it was October. You know how it is in October. Everbody is a-filling all the jugs and kegs full of scuppernong wine and bullice wine. Muscadine? We says 'bullice.' Well, anyways this man call them wild black grape. Uncle was staying to Cousin Jake's house and Jake always was a great hand to make wine. The Law never did stop you from making some to keep in the barn for sickness. And the deacon didn't refuse when Jake told him to sample his. Seems like he musta been needing some medicine. He sampled two kinds. He musta sampled pretty gentrous. And here he started home and walking by old Salem Church on the old River Road, sleep just naturally over-powered him. Now coach-whip does their running and lashing in May. One wraps around you and holds you down while the other does the lashing. They're not supposed to run nobody in the fall but the next thing he knew a big coach-whip had him tied up to a big log and was whistling for another one to come and lay on the lashing. My cousin John told us that Man's Uncle showed all the stripes that night. They were still red stripes. His wife had him in bed and was pouring black coffee down him.

Zackie Knox
As told to Genevieve W. Chandler, WPA field worker.
Murrells Inlet, South Carolina 1937.

∾ ℘

The Governor and the Pirates

During Governor Robert Johnson's tenure the pirate Blackbeard felt strong enough to defy the government. His four ships, sailing under the flag of skull and crossbones, were frightening monsters when they sailed into the Charles Town harbor. The pirates were every bit as fearful and shocking as the pirate vessels. Blackbeard looked ferocious with his abundant beard plaited and adorned with hemp. When the hemp was torched, smoke encircled Blackbeard's face. No person in his right mind desired to face such a man in a showdown. One day Blackbeard quickly maneuvered a ploy. He captured Samuel Wragge and his four-year-old son and held them hostage. Blackbeard's men needed drugs and he promised not to kill the Wragges if Governor Johnson sent the medicines.

The Wragge family, prominent English people, settled in Charles Town and they owned property in other vicinities. When Governor Johnson got word of their capture he was in a quandary. The last thing he wanted to do was make a deal with Blackbeard, but realizing that the pirate would behead his prisoners if the drugs were not delivered, the governor sent the medicines to the buccaneers. Afterwards, the Wragges were stripped of their clothing and money and left on a raw wind-swept island. When they were discovered, the governor set his mind on getting Blackbeard. But his booty turned out to be Stede Bonnet, another of the most bloodthirsty pirates in the business. Bonnet had learned his craft from Blackbeard and his ship had joined the Bonnet group in the Cape Fear region.

Colonel William Rhett, who occupied the post of Receiver-General of the province, and lived in Charles Town, met with Governor Johnson. Rhett pointed out that Bonnet had but one ship, and he knew where it was at that moment. They set up a plan. Whereas Bonnet had one sloop with ten guns and sixty men, Colonel Rhett would lead two sloops and overtake him. Rhett's ships, the *Sea Nymph*, with eight guns and a crew of sixty men, and the *Henry*, the largest of the ships with eight guns and seventy men, left Charles Town with a flourish. On September 10, 1718, Governor Johnson and many others were there to wish Colonel Rhett Godspeed. The *Sea Nymph* and the *Henry* proceeded to Sullivan's Island to make final preparations for the voyage to Cape Fear.

On September 27, as the ships neared Cape Fear, Rhett, looking through his spyglass, spotted the *Royal James*, Bonnet's ship. Rhett's ship also had been detected. Blasts of cannons thundered through the air.

Suddenly the people on Rhett's ships figured out the plan of attack from Bonnet. They realized that the pirate had not been in the business very long, and he was not the most skilled person at the logistics of war. The pirates likely would maintain a running conflict with the hope that they would find an opening to the sea and make an escape. Just as Colonel Rhett had expected, Bonnet's ship charged. As Rhett's ships responded, all three ships ran aground on a sand bar. Unfortunately, the deck of the *Royal James* was turned away from the *Henry*, while every inch of the *Henry* was mercilessly lying bare. Regardless of the situation, both ships entered a bloody contest. It seemed the pirates would win. Some of them went so far as to remove their hats and bow to the enemy. Late in the day, when the tide lifted the sloops from their stranded positions, a flag of truce was received and the *Royal James* surrendered unconditionally. The people of Charles Town waited anxiously for details of the battle. Finally they spotted Colonel Rhett's ships coming into the harbor. Ten men were killed and fourteen wounded on the *Henry*. Two were killed and four wounded on the *Sea Nymph*. Seven of the pirate crew were killed and five wounded, two of whom died soon afterwards.

Before and After Freedom

Stede Bonnet and twenty of his men were tried by Judge Nicholas Trott and publicly hanged at White Point, their bodies were left dancing in the wind as a caution to others interested in piracy. Bonnet's men were laid to rest in the marsh below the low water mark. Not that the events of that fall forever ended the deeds of the pirates

In his offices in Charles Town on a Sunday morning during the next month, Governor Robert Johnson paced rapidly back and forth, muttering to himself. He had just received some very disturbing news. A notorious pirate named Moody had been sighted off the bar with a vessel carrying fifty guns and two hundred men. "These devils have troubled us long enough," explained the governor, banging his fist on the able. "They must be stopped at any cost."

He called a meeting of his council. He told them of the danger of invasion by the pirates. He said that many appeals had been made to England for a battleship to guard the harbor, but nothing had been done about it. The Carolina coast was unprotected. A pirate gang could sail up the harbor and land in front of the Custom House in Charles Town before a single thing could be done to stop them. The citizens still lived in fear. The colony's valuable trade would soon be ruined, with the sea-robbers seizing and plundering all merchant ships coming or going.

All of these things the governor told his council. They knew he spoke the truth. He stood tall and straight before them and cried, "Gentlemen, the time has come for the colony to defend itself. We must send an armed fleet against this invader, and we must do it now."

The council, which was composed of the oldest and most experienced men in the colony, declared that they would start at once to get together a force that would stand up against this Moody and his fifty guns.

At this time, there were about twenty trading vessels in the harbor, waiting to be loaded with merchandise for the markets across the water. Governor Johnson called for volunteers to man the ships and promised them all the booty they could take. Then there was the question, "Who will command the fleet?" All eyes were turned to Colonel William Rhett, who had boldly captured Stede Bonnet and his pirate crew. But Colonel Rhett had quarreled with the governor and flatly refused to have anything to do with the expedition.

"Faith, then, I shall lead the fleet myself," shouted the young governor, with flushed cheeks and flashing eyes, as he faced the cheering crowd in the council chamber.

The news spread quickly. It caused a huge sensation. "Think of it," someone exclaimed, "the governor himself going out after pirates." No one had ever heard of such a thing before. Men were filled with new confidence. Within a few days, three hundred volunteers were on board the ships awaiting orders to sail.

Then something happened that held up the expedition for about a week. The ship owners were not willing to risk losing their ships. They wanted some security from the government. Governor Johnson saw the justice of this. He called an extra session of the Assembly and laid the case before it. The Assembly voted a bill to take care of all losses and expenses the ship owners might incur.

Meanwhile, two scout boats cruised along the island shores at the entrance to the harbor with orders to stop any ship that tried to get into port. At the same time, all shipping was stopped.

Several days before the vessels of the fleet were ready for sea, the scout boats off Sullivan's Island sighted a ship and a sloop dropping anchor off the bar. For three days the strange craft lay at their moorings, making no suspicious move.

At midnight on November 4th, Governor Johnson's fleet sailed down the harbor and anchored several hundred yards below Fort Johnson, which commanded the main entrance to the port. Under cover of darkness, the vessels found their anchorage places without even being detected by the pirates.

They lay quiet all night. As the gray mists of early morning crept slowly over the sea, Governor Johnson, from the deck of his flagship, the *Mediterranean*, signaled his fleet to weigh anchor and follow him. The commander of each vessel had his orders to make no warlike display until the right moment. "They'll believe we are merchant ships and take us for easy prey," said the governor.

The *Mediterranean* steered in the direction of the pirates, with the other three ships close at her heels. All guns were under cover and the men below decks.

By eight o'clock, the governor's volunteers were close to the enemy. The trick worked. The pirates hauled in their anchors, hoisted their black flag and moved in toward the mouth of the harbor to block off retreat.

On the deck of the sloop, a big fellow, with a booming voice, long mustache and rolling eyes, stood with legs a-kimbo and called on the *King William* to surrender.

Just at that minute, Governor Johnson ran the King's colors up to the masthead of the *Mediterranean*, threw open his portholes and sent a broadside thundering over the decks of the irate sloop. Down dropped the big fellow. A dozen of his comrades were also killed by the blast. Before the others could recover from the shock, the two ships bore down upon them, and the battle began.

The hatches flew open, the men poured from below decks, their weapons pointed, while all seventy of the fleet's guns sent broadside after broadside into the pirate vessels which were now hemmed in between the shore and the open sea. The pirate ship's master got her out of this dangerous position, and made all sail to get away.

Johnson signaled the *Sea Nymph* and the *Royal James* to look after the sloop, while the *Mediterranean* and the *King William* set out in hot pursuit after the pirate ship, which seemed to have a good chance to get away.

Before and After Freedom

The pirate sloop, the *New York Revenge*, carried six guns and forty men. She tried hard to reach the open sea, but the *Royal James* and the *Sea Nymph* had her cornered. It has been said that the pirates defended themselves with bravery worthy of a better cause. For four hours, with the vessels almost yard-arm to yard-arm they kept up the fiercest struggle ever known in these waters.

On the decks, the attacking party made quick work of the pirates. In a short time, every man, including the chief, who fought to the death with the fury of a lion, was either killed or disabled. The boarding crew was in undisputed possession of the ship.

Twelve husky fellows who had abandoned their guns and fled into the hold, surrendered without a struggle. A few hours later the sloop was towed triumphantly into Charleston.

The battle took place almost within sight of Charles Town, the boom of the guns echoing across the bay. The wharves were lined with throngs of excited people, watching through spyglasses. Cheers went up as the *Sea Nymph* and the *Royal James* rounded into the harbor, the royal ensign flying at their mastheads, signaling their victory.

Governor Johnson's *Mediterranean* and the *King William* had a long, hard chase after the fleeing pirate ship. They did not come up to her until the middle of the afternoon. During the chase the pirate vessel gave up trying to defend herself. All she wanted was to get away. But Governor Johnson's ships were the fastest sailers. As soon as they came within range, the *King William* opened fire.

The first shot raked the deck of the ship, killing two of the crew. The pirates hauled down their flag and surrendered.

Led by the governor, the crew of the *Mediterranean* boarded the pirate ship. They soon had the captain and his companions fast in irons.

"We'll see what's below," said the governor.

When the hatches were opened, the Carolinians were speechless with amazement, for the hold of the ship was full of women, thirty-six of them, huddled together like lost sheep.

The ship had been bound from London to Virginia, carrying these women, who were covenant servants, and about seventy convicts. She had been captured by the pirate sloop and her name was changed from the *Eagle* to the *New York Revenge's Revenge*. She was then fitted out as a tender. Most of the crew and some of the convicts agreed to join the pirates. Those who refused to do this were held as prisoners.

When the governor got back to Charles Town he was greatly surprised to find that the captured vessels did not belong to Moody at all and had no connection with him. The commander of the pirates, killed on the sloop, proved to be another dangerous pirate named Richard Worley, who had been terrifying the New York and Pennsylvania coasts for weeks.

Naturally, the governor was proud of having wiped out this dangerous company of outlaws, but where was Moody? Perhaps he was hovering within the headlands of the neighboring harbors, waiting for a chance to do more mischief. To guard against this, Governor Johnson kept his fleet always ready for action, until he was satisfied that there was nothing to fear from this fellow.

A few days later, the ship *Minerva* from the Maderia Isles, arrived in Charles Town. Her captain reported his ship had been taken just off the bar by Moody, who had found out about the plans being made in Charles Town to capture him. He took the *Minerva* about a hundred leagues out to sea, plundered her and then took flight.

Most of the prisoners brought into Charles Town had been dangerously wounded, and the authorities hastened to have them condemned to death and hanged before they could die of their injuries and thus cheat the gallows.

Judge Nicholas Trott ordered that the convicts and covenant servants should be sold for their terms of service and the money was divided—one-half to the captors and one-half to the owners of the ships.

The power of the outlaws of the sea was broken by the victory over them by the Carolinians. Two of the most ruthless freebooters on the coast had been taken with their crews, but the sea was still teeming with pirate craft, manned by as desperate outlaws as any of those who had been hanged at White Point in Charles Town.

Governor Johnson kept appealing to England and at last, on April 29, 1719, a huge battleship, the *Flambrough*, was riding at anchor in the harbor. The man-o-war *Phoenix* was sent to cruise along the coast, keeping a look-out for freebooters. The people of Charles Town felt safe once again.

A petition to Governor Robert Johnson petitioned him to continue his governship. His gentle and good administration was mentioned. No other person was fitter to govern, some people said. Johnson declined, saying that he held his commission from the true and absolute lords and proprietors of the province, and he knew of no power or authority that could dispossess him of the same but only those who gave him those authorities. He dissolved the Assembly, but they regrouped themselves and chose James Moore, Jr. as their governor.

WPA reporters including Irma L. Bennett and C.S. Murray.
Charleston, South Carolina 1940.

Before and After Freedom

Sandy Claw and Uncle Sam

When I was little I thought Sandy Claw and Uncle Sam were the two best things in the world. I thought Sandy Claw was giving you all them things your Mama had to pay for. And I thought Uncle Sam was a good man too. I thought he was sitting up there in his office in Conway and I thought when you paid your taxes Uncle Sam just saved it all for you. And when you needed money I just thought you could go right there to Uncle Sam and get your money. Uncle Sam's picture was so ugly. I don't think Uncle Sam was so good to make you buy the land and keep on paying the tax. I called that no business.

Now the meanest thing in the world? I thought that was the policeman. I saw him catch his own people and rush them off to jail. I saw them run down a man and arrest him. Policemen ran him down and cut a cross on the front of him. The sheriff and policeman can sure be rough on you.

Maude Esther Lee Pickett
As told to Genevieve W. Chandler, WPA field worker.
Georgetown County, South Carolina.

The Mail Boat

You hear about Lizzie Russell? It happened before her first child come and she was wanting to go to Georgetown to see her aunt. So she took her clothes in one of them handle baskets and footed it to Wachesaw Landing and got on the boat. She stayed out half her visit and her aunt said she got up early on the day for the boat to run and came out with her basket packed up and a box of new things she had bought in town and said she just had to be a-getting home. Said she left word for Esau to meet her on every boat because she didn't know for sure which day she was going to make it back.

When Esau met Lizzie that day she came off that mail boat a-toting that first child off that boat in that basket. They wouldn't carry women that way no more on the boat nor train nor nothing. They made a new law since that day.

She name that first child Mail Boat. I wondered how some people gave him such a name and I was grown up before I heard Grandma and Grandpa talking one day about Mail Boat Russell.

As told to Genevieve W. Chandler, WPA field worker.
Murrells Inlet, South Carolina.

Hiding from the Yankees

I'm Ellen Godfrey. I was born at Longwood Plantation on the Waccamaw River in 1837. During the Confedrick War we had to flee the Yankees. We were put on a boat and flatted up to Marlboro County. Three hundred head o' people been on boat. Flat 'em all up to Marlboro. Two weeks going up. Couldn't pull we clothes off while on flat boat. Boat name of Riprey. *A woman on boat drop her baby and give him name of Riprey. We cook on the flat. Bank up dirt. Fire will make on dirt. Put big pot on fire. Cook. Fry meat. Bake. Pile coals on top and logs or planks across the top with earth on top of the planks. On this great bed of coals the oven could be heated for baking. Oven? Oven was a great iron skillet like vessel with three legs and a snug lid. The oven on the boat baked biscuit, pound cake. Put your buttermilk biscuit in, lid on, and pile live-oak coals on top. You had to be one of the ones who had done this a long time to know when to take the lid off. When we come to the Pee Dee River we get off flat. Go in gentleman's barn. He turn the bridge. Been there a week.*

Go back on boat and get to Marlboro. Doctor come on boat. Doctor name of Lane. White lady come and tend to the women. We were put in wagon and carried to the street (slave quarters). Major Drake's plantation. He had one son, Pete Drake. Wife was a little bit of a woman.

Clothes gone to wash that morning. Can't go out. Clothes gone.

We were taken to dirt camp to stay in, to hide from Yankee. Dirt piled up like a potato hill. Pile 'em. Have a street row of houses in dirt camp. We in dirt camp.

My loom put at door. I been there and weaving. Six looms on that side. Six looms on this side. I see the Yankees a-coming. Wearing hats with crown as high as a walking stick. I talk with Abraham Lincoln's own son, Johnny, and bless your heart I glad for Freedom.

Maussa been hiding. Been in swamp. All the old men, too old for the army, hid in Marlboro swamps and were fed by slaves until Yankees passed on.

Yankee officer come. "Where Maham Ward and John J. Woodward? Tell them to come and take these people out of the dirt camp. Put them in flat. Carry back home."

Going home we cooked all night. Rice. Tater. Collard. Cornbread. Give us a quilt to put over our head. I sleep. I sleep in the cotton. I roost up in the cotton. Rooted it up and burrowed down. It was December. Winter time. Easier coming home. Going up against the current, only poles and cant hooks, tedious going.

Got home. Mother Molly dead on flat. Bury she right at Longwood graveyard.

My last days are happy days. 'Mancipation!

Ellen Godfrey
As told to Genevieve W. Chandler, WPA field worker.
Murrells Inlet, South Carolina.

∿ ∽

The Man Who Could See Ghosts

My name is Thomas Goodwater, and I was born on January 15, 1855 at Maussa Lias Winning's plantation on the Cooper River. My ma and pa been named Anjuline and Thomas Goodwater. Ma had eight boys and eights gals.

There was a family doctor on the plantation named of James Hibbins. My eye used to run water a lot and he take out my eye and couldn't put it back in. That is why I am blind now. The doctor asked my pa not to say anything about it 'cause he would lose his job. Maussa Winning never knew the truth of my blindness.

There used to be dances almost every week and the older boys and gals walked twelve miles to be there. Sometime there was a tambourine beater, sometime they used an old wash tub and beat it with wood sticks and sometime they just slapped their hands. When anyone died they were buried in the morning or early afternoon.

I always could see ghosts because I was born with a caul on my face. Anybody born with a caul over the face can see ghosts. A person born with a caul over the face has second sight and can see strange things that normal people can't see. I can see them just as plain as ever. Sometimes I see a ghost I know and other times I see a ghost I don't know. I can see their feet because they walk with their feet off the ground. My sister used to put sand on the fire and then I wouldn't see any ghosts for a good while. One day my uncle was passing a church and a ghost appeared on the porch. My uncle had a dog with him. He started to run and the dog started to run, and down the road they went. He say he ran so fast that the wind had his shirt-tail stiff as a board. He couldn't outrun the dog, nor could the dog outrun him.

Thomas Goodwater
As told to Augustus Ladson, WPA field worker.
Charleston, South Carolina.

∿ ∽

The Slave Who Witnessed History

My name is Elijah Green. I was born in Charleston at 82 King Street on December 25, 1863. The house is still there. Recent owner is Judge Whaley. From the southeast of what was Boundary Street to the Battery was the city limit and from the northwest of Boundary Street for several miles

was nothing but farm land. All my brothers were farm hands for our maussa, George W. Jones. I did all the house work until the war when I was given to William Jones as his "daily gift."

As the daily gift of Maussa William H Jones I had to go to Virginia during the war. In the battle of Richmond General Lee had General Grant almost beaten. He drove him almost in the Potomac River and then took seven pieces of his artillery. When General Grant saw how near defeat he was, he put up a white flag as a signal for time out to bury his dead. That flag staid up for three weeks while General Grant was digging trenches. In the meantime he got a message to President Lincoln asking him to send a reinforcement of soldiers. General Sherman was in charge of the regiment who sent word to General Grant to hold his position until he had captured Columbia and Savannah and burned out Charleston while on his way with the dispatch of 45,000 men. When General Sherman got to Virginia the battle was renewed and continued for seven days at the end of which General Lee surrendered to General Grant. During the seven days fight the battle got so hot that Maussa William Jones made his escape and it was two days before I knew he was gone. One of the Generals sent me home and I got here in two days before Maussa got home. He went up in the attic and stayed there until the war ended. I carried all his meals to him and told him all the news. Maussa was a frightened man and I was sorry for him. That battle of Richmond, Virginia was the worst in American history.

My Maussa ran a blockade. He had ships roaming the sea to capture pirate ships. He had an overseer who took care of everything on the twenty-five acres in Charleston. The overseer blew the horn, which was a conch shell, at six in the morning and every person had better answer when the roll was called at seven.

Not until John C. Calhoun's body was carried down Boundary Street was the name changed in his honor. He is buried in St. Phillip's churchyard, with a laurel tree planted at his head. Four men and me dug his grave and I cleared the spot where his monument stands. The monument was put up by Pat Collington, a Charleston mason.

A group of white men were in Doctor Wilson's drugstore one day when I went to buy something. They commenced to ask me questions concerning some historical happenings and I answered them all. Dr. Wilson bet me that I couldn't tell who fired the first shot on Fort Sumter. I told him I did know and he offered a dollar if I was right. I told him I wasn't going to tell unless the dollar was given to one of the men. He did so and I told them it was Edward Ruffin who fired the first shot and the dollar was mine. I went on to explain that Anderson was determined not to leave Fort Sumter but when about four shells had hit the Fort he was glad to be able to come out. When Sherman was coming through Columbia, he fired and a shell lodged in the southeast end of the State House which was forbidden to be fixed. He was coming down Main Street when that happened.

Elijah Green
As told to Augustus Ladson, WPA field worker.
Charleston, South Carolina.

Before and After Freedom

Never Had Time to Play Games

When the gun shoot on Hilton Head Island, I been twenty-two years old. Pa was Tony MacKnight and he belonged to Massau Stephen Elliott. Ma went by the name of Venus MacKnight and she belonged to Maussa Joe Eddings, who had a plantation on Parris Island. The overseer on that plantation been Edward Blunt. He been poor white trash but he worked hard and saved his money. He bought Ma and brought her to Beaufort to work in the house by the Baptist Church. I had seven brothers name of Jacob, Tony, Robert, Moses, and I can't remember the others. I had one sister, Eliza.

When I been a little gal, I worked in the house. Worked all day. I polished knife and fork, made bed, sweep floor, never had time to play games. When I got bigger, they sent me to school to Missus Crocker to learn to be a seamstress.

When I was small, I slept on the floor in Missus Blunt's room. I ate the food she left on the table. They never learned me to read and write. I ain't have time for such thing. I go to church at the Baptist Church. Had to sit upstairs and the white folks sat downstairs. When I got sick they sent for a doctor and he tended me.

They had a jail in Beaufort and it was run by Mr. McGraw. If a person been too bad like run in the street and thing, he get put in jail and Mr. McGraw lick 'em. I been locked in jail one time. They hung me up by my wrist and beat me twenty-five licks with a cowhide strap.

When the Yankee come the Blunts left Beaufort, and I went back to Parris Island. Then I came back to Beaufort and worked in the gin house. The Yankee pay me for work and I took my money and bought twenty acres of land on Parris Island. I ain't have that land now because the Government take 'em for heself and made me move. The Government built a naval station on my land.

Does I hate Mr. Blunt? No, I ain't hate 'em. He was poor white trash but he's dead now.

Lucretia Heyward
As told to Chlotilde Martin, WPA field worker.
Beaufort, South Carolina.

∾ ∾

Aunt Hetty Was Something Else

Aunt Hetty was something else. She held her head high as a crane. Straight as if she had a board in her neck. She was a pain. Her grandchild died and she said, "Got that much off my hands." Aunt Hetty said that! And if you ever made her mad...

She raised Rina, Mary, Janie, Becca, Julie and Frank. One son. Frank died and left her one grandchild. It was little and sickly, puny. Well, the baby died. Every time a member of Aunt Hetty's family died, she said, "By King and by Heaven, I did all I could for 'em."

After Sarah died, Aunt Hetty said, "By King and by Heaven, I got that much off my hands."

The time came for Aunt Hetty to go. Us say we'll do all we can for Aunt Hetty. She was a-lying in her bed and I fan and I fan. I spend the whole day fanning Aunt Hetty. Then she was gone. Us laugh and say, "By King and By Heaven, we did all we could and got that much off our hands."

As told to Genevieve W. Chandler, WPA field worker.
Murrells Inlet, South Carolina.

Funerals Were at Night

I was born in Adams Run on January 21, 1844. My father was Robert King; my mother was Minder King.

There was a meeting house on the plantation in which we used to have meetings every Chuseday night, Wednesday night, and Thursday night. Dr. Jerico was the pastor. All the black folks went to church on Sunday 'cause they didn't have any work to do for Maussa. Grandma taught the Catechism and how to sing.

Funerals were held at night and when we were ready to go to the graveyard everybody would light a pine knot as a torch. This is one of the songs we sang:

Going to carry this body
To the graveyard
Graveyard don't you know me?
To lay this body down.

The Yankees took three nights to march through and I was afraid of them and climbed a tree. One called me down and he say, "I am your friend." He gave me a piece of money and I wasn't afraid no more.

Adele Frost
As told to Hattie Mobley, WPA field worker.
Adams Run, South Carolina.

I Stopped Shaking Hands and Kissing

My pa belonged to a man on Edisto Island. Pa's name was Adam Collins but he took his maussa's name when Maussa made Pa the coachman. One day Pa did something and his maussa whipped him. The next day, which was Monday, Pa carried Maussa about four miles from home in the woods and gave him the same amount of licking he was given on Sunday. Pa tied him to a tree and unhitched the horse so it couldn't get tied up and kill himself. Pa went to the landing and caught a boat to Charleston. He went to the Charleston waterfront and asked for a job on a ship so he could get up North. He got a job and sailed with the ship. Back at Edisto, they searched the island and tracked Pa to the landing and they thought Pa had drowned.

When the war began we were taken to Aiken. The Yankees were coming. You could see balls flying through the air when Sherman was coming. Bombs hit trees in our yard. I was on my knees scrubbing when I was told I was free. I was so glad. In the days of slavery women were just given time enough to deliver their babies. They delivered a baby about eight in the morning and at twelve had to be back to work.

I like Abraham Lincoln. Since Lincoln shook hands with his assassin who shot him, I stopped shaking hands, even in church, and I don't believe in kissing neither. That carries meanness. Maussa was betrayed by one of his bosom friends with a kiss.

Susan Hamilton
As told to Augustus Ladson, WPA field worker.
Charleston, South Carolina.

Epilogue

Nothing I write can be accomplished alone. I could never have written this book without the generous help of the Director of the South Caroliniana Library at the University of South Carolina, Columbia Herbert J. Hartsook and his staff including: Henry Fulmer, Graham Duncan, Beth Bilderback, Brian Cuthrell, Robin Copp, Beverly Bullock and Ashley Bowden. Graham, especially, must have lost weight as he delivered dozens if not hundreds of WPA files to my station and returned them to their place of safekeeping. My husband Sid played a major role in putting quarters in the parking meters and paying the fees when they read EXPIRED. From their home in Charlotte, North Carolina to their boat in the South Carolina Lowcountry, Garry and Shirlene Rhyne were on call twenty-four hours a day for computer help. The debt I owe Kirsten Sutton for her idea for this book for the History Press is incalculable, and kudos to her staff for editing the manuscript. All of the above deserve more credit than I can give in this simple statement.

Nancy Rhyne

Index

About the Author

For almost twenty-five years Nancy and her husband Sid have traveled and explored the back roads and the people of coastal South Carolina and Georgia. Nancy has written twenty books focusing on the myth and history of the South. She has been awarded first-place prizes for two of her books by a panel from the University of South Carolina College of Journalism. She has also been cited for her work to promote literacy by speaking at over seventy-five South Carolina schools. Longtime residents of Myrtle Beach, Nancy and Sid now live in Columbia, South Carolina.